UNDERSTANDING
AD HD

Our Personal Journey

KEN & ANDREA McCLUSKEY

**PORTAGE &
MAIN PRESS**

Printed and bound in Canada by Kromar Printing Ltd.

01 02 03 04 05 5 4 3 2 1

Portage & Main Press acknowledges the financial support of the Government of Canada through the Book Publishing Industry Development Program (BPIDP) for our publishing activities.

National Library of Canada Cataloguing in Publication Data

McCluskey, Ken W. (Kenneth Wilfred), 1949-

    Understanding ADHD

    Includes bibliographical references.
    ISBN 1-894110-93-5

1. Attention-deficit hyperactivity disorder. 2. Attention-deficit-disordered children.
I. McCluskey, Andrea. II. Title.

RJ506.H9M32 2001   618.92'8589   C2001-910624-6

Book and Cover Design by Gallant Design Ltd.
Photographs of Amber Densley (front and back cover)
by Thomas Fricke
Cartoons by William H. Stevens

PORTAGE &
MAIN PRESS

100-318 McDermot Avenue
Winnipeg, Manitoba, Canada R3A 0A2
E-mail: books@peguis.com
Tel: 1-204-987-3500
Toll-Free: 1-800-667-9673
Fax: 1-866-734-8477

It isn't all that hard to provide a warm, caring, happy environment for your children if you've grown up in a warm, caring, happy environment yourself. Each of us did. Once again, we dedicate this book to

Wilf & Yeary McCluskey

and

Oliver and Anna Parisian

for being such wonderful parents for us, such wonderful grandparents for Chris and Amber, and such wonderful great grandparents for Kristjana, Kailynd, Kadynce, Hunter, and Easton.

Contents

FOREWORD

O n a glorious, warm, sunny September Saturday in 1999, Amber McCluskey was married. As is usually the case with weddings, the bride was beautiful, the groom was proud, and family and friends were present to celebrate the important event. Now, it goes without saying that weddings are special, marker events in the lives of those who have come together to create a new family unit. In this same way, Amber's wedding was special. It is also fair to say, however, that Amber's wedding was special in another way. It was one more triumphant step in a journey toward adult responsibilities—a journey characterized by far more roadblocks than most young women experience. The years leading up to this major moment in her life story were not easy for Amber, her parents, or her brother. Amber had grown up as a "classic" ADHD child, with extremely impulsive motor behavior, difficulty staying on task, and short attention span.

Understanding ADHD: Our Personal Journey is a lively, personal account of the life of Amber, and the trials and tribulations her parents and older brother Chris have had to face in attempting to cope with her attention-deficit/hyperactivity disorder. This book is extraordinary for several reasons, which no doubt accounts for its tremendous success in its previous incarnation as *Butterfly Kisses*. Although ADHD is a timely issue, most authors typically approach the topic from an objective perspective and recount the most up-to-date research in a style designed for an audience of academics and practitioners. In contrast, *Understanding ADHD* is a firsthand account of living with an ADHD child from the perspective of the parents. It could well have been written as an academic treatise, since both Ken and Andrea are well versed in the literature in the field. They chose instead to present their personal experience, a subjective account of life with Amber, written in a style that is warm, engaging, and filled with humor. What they also managed to do, however, was to ground the book in the literature in a way that ensured it would have broad audience appeal. Above all, they wrote a book that is accessible to those who need it the most: parents, educators, and others who live and work daily with ADHD children.

In their recounting of "life with Amber", Ken and Andrea hold nothing back, and the result is somewhat of an emotional roller coaster for the reader. Although the tone of the book is, for the most part, humorous, its brutal honesty also ensures that the reader cannot escape the pain of a little girl who struggles to "fit in" and meet the expectations of peers and teachers, or the frustration and exhaustion of parents who can never relax.

Understanding ADHD is not merely a narrative, however. One of its greatest strengths lies in the many bits of advice and proven strategies that Ken and Andrea suggest for dealing with ADHD children both at home and at school. A book filled with love and hope, it focuses not on the negative, but rather on achieving and celebrating successes when parenting and teaching a child with ADHD. At another, more fundamental level, it is about the "best practice" for raising and educating any child.

In the conclusion of *Understanding ADHD*, Ken and Andrea make the following comment: "Our journey is not yet done, but we're proud of what we've wrought and of who Amber has become." Ken, Andrea, Amber, and Chris all have reason to be proud. Their journey together continues and, like every family, they have their ups and downs: moments of great happiness entwined with ones of great difficulty. The success of the earlier version of this book, while unanticipated, was certainly not unwarranted—there are many readers of that first volume who will no doubt be pleased to catch up on the most recent happenings in the lives of the McCluskey family. Obviously, Amber is now married, but there is much more to be revealed with respect to family and career developments.

Yes, the McCluskey family journey continues, and this latest version of the story confirms the hopeful outlook and the faith in the power of thinking positively. It also adds to the store of knowledge that is slowly being generated with respect to the effective ways for encouraging the development of ADHD children toward happy, productive lives as adults. In the final analysis, this is a highly readable, informative, down-to-earth book for people who are on the "front line" as parents or educators.

– Annabelle Mays, Ph.D.
   Dean of Education
   University of Winnipeg

Acknowledgments

It's not often two people have the privilege of working in two gloriously happy settings. We have been given that opportunity. We would like to thank our long-time co-workers at the Human Resource Centre in Lord Selkirk School Division and our newfound colleagues at the University of Winnipeg for the intellectual stimulation, friendship, and support they have given to us, and for the opportunities they have provided for Amber and Chris.

We must also express our appreciation to three people who, in succession, worked long and hard on this project. Sadly, we have lost two of these fine individuals since the book first appeared. Nadine Jenkins was always much more than a secretary/librarian—we viewed her almost as a co-author. After Nadine helped pull together the prototype package, Jean Lee, in her energetic and capable fashion, typed draft after draft of the manuscript. Leona Strong, now happily retired in British Columbia, arrived in time to mop up on this initiative and move on with us to several new endeavors.

Even more to the point, all three were great friends to Amber. Leona engaged the large-sized Amber during friendly visits at the Human Resource Centre. "Mama Jean" became a buddy to mid-sized Amber during sleepovers, Easter egg hunts, and dynamic socializing. And Nadine was there since the small-sized Amber period: those two bonded big time through their common interests in Shakespeare, theater, and people watching. Thanks all. We think back with great gratitude and affection to those times.

Here comes trouble! From the first,
the mouth was open.

Chapter 1

DEFINITION: A SUBJECTIVE PERSPECTIVE

When we started writing this story, our hyperactive daughter Amber was 13 years old: it took eight years before we finally completed our original book about her (McCluskey & McCluskey, 1996). By the time it finally finds its way into this most recent incarnation, she'll be only a month or so shy of her 26th birthday. From the beginning, the words did not come easily. On the one hand, this inability to get things down on paper was discouraging; we've often been troubled by the fact that we couldn't write about our own daughter in lucid fashion—so many things she did were incredibly frustrating and almost beyond description.

On the other hand, perhaps things have worked out for the best after all. Had this book come out 13 years ago, we would have been looking at Amber from the middle of the parenting process, when she was just entering her teens. Now she has survived those difficult years and grown into a young woman with a family of her own. Our current perspective is surely far more complete, and more optimistic, than it was during her adolescence. Indeed, we're a trifle surprised that Amber has made it this far—many's the time we felt tempted to put a period to her existence. However, we restrained ourselves, she gradually grew into something vibrant and special, and we feel much better about the whole situation than we did in the '70s, '80s, and early '90s.

In retrospect, one of our problems was that we began our story by trying to write an objective tome about hyperactivity, with a few "Amber examples" tossed in to make things livelier. After years of banging our heads against the wall, however, we had a flash of insight that allowed us to move along and bring some closure to our literary efforts. Specifically, because attention-deficit/hyperactivity disorder (ADHD) has become the label *du jour* in the educational and medical communities (Armstrong, 1996), there has recently been a proliferation of books, training packages, and videos on the topic—we really didn't have that much to add in the objective realm. Why simply parrot material written by others?

So we changed gears entirely and moved toward a much less elusive goal. Since objective knowing pales in comparison to subjective living, we decided to dispense with the scientific approach and focus instead on what it is like to parent and grow (age might be a better word) with an ADHD youngster. With Amber having long passed through her adolescence, physically if not mentally, we feel equipped to discuss some of the strategies we've used to help her to this point in the journey. To put it another way, we are hoping that a personalized, feeling book with personalized, real-life examples and suggestions might prove more helpful to parents and educators than one more "The facts ma'am, just the facts" text.

This is not to say that we won't strive to be thorough and scholarly. Any serious attempt to understand ADHD must involve a consideration of the literature and research. However, our intent is to move toward personal situations and solutions. To this end, although we do cite many sources that have been helpful to us, we have dispensed with references entirely in chapter 3—it's meant to be descriptive, experiential, and fun. And throughout, we endeavor to present useful material in a "down home", positive manner.

From the outset, we have gone about this business in a very humble, tentative manner. We don't pretend to be model parents—there are no such things. We are not so presumptuous as to offer a "how to" lecture: there is no cut-and-dried, correct way to parent a hyperactive child, or indeed, any child. What works for one parent or teacher with one child in one setting may not work in a different situation with different players. We learned early to beware of "experts" bearing advice; people who are sure they are right usually are not. For us, parenting is a process, with an up and down, ebb and flow to it, rather than a set of definitive techniques. Since there are no simplistic, arbitrarily correct answers, the true art of parenting is the flexibility to adjust to new and continually changing circumstances. Our approach is likely to be unsatisfying for those who are seeking cookbook solutions. When it comes to parenting, we regard ourselves not as chefs, but as novices experimenting in the kitchen. The one thing we are sure about, though, is that a malleable, adaptable approach is the way to go, particularly when dealing with a hyper youngster like Amber.

While we don't wish to appear cynical or to belabor the point, some children raised by so-called "experts" turn out to be "little monsters". The world today is plagued by people who give advice, despite the fact that they can't keep their own houses in order. We are here to tell you that our house is in disarray—we just do the best we can. To highlight the difference between fantasy and day-to-day reality, both of us loathed, despised, and abhorred the thought of physical punishment of any kind—until we had to deal with Amber. While we still don't like it, we have, on rare occasion, resorted to spanking. Our idealistic philosophy had to be modified somewhat in light of the reality of Amber's extremely recalcitrant, dangerous childhood behavior.

Incidentally, we acknowledge that it is impossible to generalize from one child to an entire population. Many of the examples and incidents here are naturally idiosyncratic to Amber. Still, we are convinced that using a case study, Amberesque approach will make the whole issue of hyperactivity come alive with a vengeance. In short, we are presenting an imperfect, "warts-and-all" situation, not a magical, fictional one. Amber is a real, living, breathing, emotional individual; we hope this will be a real, emotive book that adds a slice-of-life dimension to the field.

Dismissing Definitive Definitions

Although we have pledged to take a subjective look at hyperactivity, it would be limiting to avoid technical information completely; there are some facts that must be addressed. Since we're not experts by any means, we'll simply offer a quick overview of the area from our perspective. For practitioners interested in an in-depth consideration of various aspects of ADHD, there are excellent texts available (Barkley, 1998; Goldstein & Goldstein, 1998; Maté, 1999; Phelan, 1993; Weyandt, 2001).

Perusing DSM-II, DSM-III, DSM-III-R, and DSM-IV, the various revisions of the *Diagnostic and Statistical Manual of Mental Disorders* (American Psychiatric Association, 1968, 1980, 1987, 1994)—the Bible of diagnosis as it were—it is clear that definitions of hyperactivity have shifted and evolved over the years. In different times and places, terms such as *hyperkinetic reaction of childhood, minimal brain dysfunction, minimal brain damage, hyperactivity, attention deficit disorder (ADD) with or without hyperactivity,* and *attention-deficit/hyperactivity disorder (ADHD)* have been used.

Most definitions, past and present, focus on behavior such as distractibility, impulsivity, motor restlessness, short attention span, and the need to seek stimulation. The idea that the disorder can manifest itself in different forms really took hold in DSM-III, which made the distinction between ADD with hyperactivity and ADD without hyperactivity. In both cases, the disorganization, difficulty staying on task, and short attention span are present. However, these two subtypes of ADD are distinguished by the fact that the former usually features extremely impulsive motor activity (such as excessive fidgeting, climbing, running, restlessness during sleep, and the inability to stay seated), while the latter does not. In other words, ADD with hyperactivity describes what has classically been thought of as a "hyper" child; ADD without hyperactivity recognizes that mental underfocusing and attentional problems may be present even when the body is relatively still.

In DSM-III-R, ADD with and without hyperactivity were in fact recombined into the single ADHD classification. The contributors to DSM-IV, however—again grappling with the need to differentiate among various forms of this multi-faceted disorder—identified three specific subtypes of ADHD (attention-deficit/hyperactivity disorder, predominantly hyperactive-impulsive type; attention-deficit/hyperactivity disorder, predominantly inattentive type; and attention-deficit/hyperactivity disorder, combined type). To be on the safe side, when no one is really quite sure what is going on, there is also the ambiguous ADHD "not otherwise specified" category.

Although we wouldn't quarrel with the fact that all these conditions exist (often as entirely separate disorders), we are concerned that the DSM-III category of ADD without hyperactivity became, and has remained, a catch-all in some quarters. While we are not necessarily opposed to using medication judiciously and appropriately to treat ADHD, in our view, the blurring of the distinction between mental and physical hyperactivity has sometimes resulted in misdiagnosis and overuse and abuse of some drugs. In the past, before a diagnosis of hyperactivity was made, there would usually be clear, excessive physical activity, plus many other signs. Now, it is painfully easy to miss the mark and conclude that many passive children are suffering from some form of ADD or ADHD. Some undoubtedly have major attentional problems (and would fall, quite legitimately, into the current ADHD, predominantly inattentive classification), but look at the potential for error: a quiet child who drifts off task, an incipiently creative daydreamer, a plain old shy kid, an underachiever, a troubled youngster whose anxieties are getting in the way of focusing, or an abuse victim might all be easily misdiagnosed. For this reason, a diagnosis of ADHD should only be made by qualified practitioners in the area, and even then only after careful observation, thorough consideration of the circumstances, and intensive consultation with parents and educators.

Every now and again, we are tempted to ask if anyone really knows what constitutes ADHD; it appears to mean very different things to different people (and different things to the same people at different times). It is one thing to be current, but—when definitions change in seemingly willy-nilly fashion—it does raise doubts, at least in our minds. Are researchers fine-tuning diagnostic categories to lead to more specific and better treatment? Or are they floundering, becoming too "picky", and shifting direction indiscriminately? Was DSM-III or DSM-III-R off-base? Is DSM-IV? What will DSM-V bring in this new millennium?

It is risky business to attempt to specify definitive classification and diagnostic categories (cf. Carlson & Rapport, 1989; Johnson, 1989). Because Amber fits the most current definition of ADHD, combined type, it makes sense for us to zero in here. When all is said and done, however, we prefer to think of hyperactivity in the old, classic sense. Worrying about precise semantics can be left to the authorities in the field. In our informal fashion, we will use terms such as *hyperactivity, overactivity, ADD*, and *ADHD* virtually synonymously and interchangeably to refer to the traditionally hyperactive child (who exhibits both mental and motor restlessness). We also accept Melmed's (2001) contention that hyperactivity is generally not a happy condition: ADHD children, adolescents, and adults usually find that behaviors associated with the disorder interfere with important parts of their lives and cause a pronounced degree of social-emotional pain and suffering.

Of course, there must be some flexibility in definition—not every hyperactive child will necessarily show specific traits at all times. And many "normal" youngsters can exhibit characteristics of ADHD on occasion without being hyperactive. When push comes to shove, we don't really care all that much about definition. While researchers argue back and forth about terms, we have a hyper daughter, and we have to cope. Parents tend to worry less about definition and more about making life bearable.

Introducing Amber (and Supporting Cast)

One should always begin with positives, so we'll start by saying that Amber is a delight. We love her dearly, but wonder why we continually have to remind ourselves of the fact. In an effort to describe what we have been through, we will discuss Amber's past, her formative years, the present, and—with cautious optimism—the future as we envision it. Although we are extremely encouraged by recent trends, we're too weary and wary to celebrate yet—there's still some work to be done.

To set the stage, we should mention that Mom (Andrea) was a young, divorced single parent with two children: Christopher, born in 1974, and Amber, who arrived in September of the following year. Dad (Ken) came on the scene in 1977, but—after meeting Amber—it took him quite some time to work up the courage to make a lasting commitment. In the end, he did; the marriage took place in July, 1983.

From day one, Amber was an amazing problem. Sleep disturbances, unfocused behavior, and rampant overactivity highlighted her early years. As is often the case, Mom understood that all was not well. She visited various doctors, insisting "There's something wrong with this kid!" Mothers of hyperactive infants frequently do realize, shortly after bringing their children home from the hospital, that something untoward is going on—especially if they have had other, more settled children. All too often, these mothers head to their family doctors, crying out for help. Not unnaturally, the doctors check out the youngsters, give them a clean bill of health, and announce that they will soon "outgrow the problem". However, often the children don't outgrow it, and the hyperactive behavior persists, sometimes into and throughout adulthood. In our case, when Amber reached her first birthday, Mom was told, "She's developing normally." The next year, the bad behavior was attributed to "The Terrible Twos". Unfortunately, the threes, the fours, the fives, and so on were all "terrible too": we knew something was amiss.

Parents of a truly hyperactive child usually realize early on that there is a problem. It has been said that symptoms of hyperactivity begin before the age of seven, but we really feel they usually surface much earlier than that—in infancy. In fact, many mothers will tell you they knew something was wrong when they were carrying the baby. Should extreme activity "hit" suddenly later in life, say at age nine or ten, we would look to other causes.

Along the same lines, we sometimes come across children who are "holy terrors" at school, but who behave well enough at home. Conversely, other children who are settled and well-behaved at school are quite disruptive on the home front. Although not everyone shares this opinion, we believe that, in both these situations, hyperactivity is not likely the problem. When a child is disruptive at school but not at home, or vice versa, we don't see it as true ADHD. For us, with classic hyperactivity, the behaviors exist regardless of the situation. In other words, the behavior patterns are not generally situation specific: parents, teachers, and people in the community experience similar problems in getting the ADHD youngster to focus, remain on task, stay seated, and behave. The kid is a handful, whatever the setting.

In our case, Mom knew that something was definitely out of whack. Years of frustration followed, where Amber was literally dragged from doctor to doctor. Help was needed, but not forthcoming. Essentially, most medical practitioners didn't seem to appreciate the incredible frustration that is involved in dealing with an Amber. This mom, for one, actually admits to thinking about child abuse. In pure exasperation, it would be only too easy to lash out and hurt this sort of youngster.

For a spell, we pursued a vague, holy grail-type quest for diagnosis. Along the way, while running the diagnostic gamut, we got our share of unhelpful labels. When she was five, Amber was given—quite inaccurately—a working diagnosis of "schizophrenia" (by a doctor in town who had the distressing habit of diagnosing almost every child as schizophrenic). We were amazed to find that our little girl, on the basis of only a 15-minute interview, was condemned to a life of being "out of contact with reality". Happily, we had the wherewithal to ignore this pronouncement and get on with our lives. However, during her early school years, we were disheartened to find that Amber had again been labeled, this time by special educators, as being "functionally illiterate"—she was never going to learn to read. Again, we had the good sense to disregard this dire prophecy and proceed as if we had a "normal" child (obviously, the best way to proceed). Shortly thereafter, the label was softened to "learning disability" (more about that later). And finally, a diagnosis of "hyperactivity"—more accurate, but probably not much more helpful—began to emerge from doctors and school personnel alike.

However, we didn't want to be like many parents we've run into, who feel their job is done once they get a diagnosis. Some people seem quite content when a label is put on their child, for it removes responsibility and, in a sense, absolves them of guilt. In the end, the label turned out to be relatively unimportant in Amber's case. Diagnosis or not, we were still faced with an amazingly difficult child, and we had to do something proactive to deal with the situation at hand.

It goes without saying that poor parenting couldn't possibly be the problem here—Amber has had very fine parenting! Only parents who have gone through it can know how demoralizing and dehumanizing it is to be in a position where doctors, teachers, relatives, and acquaintances blame you for producing a child such as Amber. Basically, it's the classic "blame the victim" response—parents are almost universally thought to be responsible for their child's negative behavior. While they frequently are, it isn't always so. Undoubtedly, we could have done some things better and, to some extent, we likely have contributed to some of Amber's problems. On the other hand, we don't believe we are the root cause—there has always been something "in" Amber that made her tough to handle. We didn't put it there during child rearing, and we've worked hard to deal with it. Still, until we gave up worrying about our reputations (which we used to have), it was difficult not to be embarrassed and defensive at the doctor's office or during parent-teacher interviews.

One point in our defense is the fact that our kids are total opposites. While Amber is an inexhaustible, going concern, Chris can often be mistaken for a lump of clay—he is incredibly laid back. To find two youngsters, both products of the same home environment, who are so different suggests that something internal is at work.

To finish up stage setting, we came together as a family with our marriage in 1983. At that time, we officially "adopted" both kids (even the biological mother was required to go through the adoption process). We took great pains to involve the little people, so while Mom and Dad signed their "big papers", the children signed their own "official" versions (which our lawyer had taken the time to draw up). During the wedding, the kids formally gave their mother away, while the bride and groom debated if it would be possible to live happily ever after without disposing of Amber.

Before the ceremony itself, it was interesting to see how differently Chris and Amber reacted to the adoption process. Amber had no problem at all with the whole thing, including the name change from Parisian to

McCluskey. For all she cared, people could call her Amber McCluskey, Amber Parisian, or other things—and they often did. For Christopher, though, the name change was an issue. He was proud of the name Parisian and afraid he would lose his grandparents on that side if he changed it. Since he doesn't listen that well, our explanations to the contrary fell on deaf ears. As the wedding date approached, we began to get nervous. With only a short time left, he was still holding firm. Finally, however, Chris came home from school one day and announced abruptly, at our dining room table, that he was finally prepared to change his name. Thrilled that we had gotten through to the little guy at last, we all began to celebrate, somewhat prematurely as it turned out. Chris dampened the proceedings by announcing that henceforth he wanted to be called Robert Parisian—he had decided to change his first, not his last, name! We finally worked things out, but we'll never forget the incident. It's one of the few times that Amber caused us less trouble than Chris.

Anyway, the festivities soon ended, and we got down to the task of raising our hyperactive child. Throughout the process, we've had to rely heavily on support from significant others, including grandparents, aunts, uncles, cousins, friends, and colleagues. We could never have made it through alone.

From tenuous kindergarten start
(with self-styled hair) (above),
to tenacious high school finish (below).

Chapter 2

CHARACTERISTICS OF HYPERACTIVE CHILDREN

I t is, in a very real sense, unfair to lump children into one big, impersonal category of faceless hyperactivity. Each child is unique, and each will, of course, exhibit some unique behavior patterns. It is also true that there are many common traits shared by youngsters diagnosed as ADHD. Although there are other ways of approaching the issue, a number of investigators have identified specific primary and secondary traits associated with classic hyperactivity. It is not always possible to differentiate among these; there is extensive overlap. Conceptually, however, the primary-secondary distinction is a neat organizational tool for looking systematically at ADHD children. Therefore, in this chapter, we consider—in soft, nondogmatic fashion—some of these primary and secondary characteristics, as well as issues such as incidence of ADHD, identification, and etiology.

Incidence

When discussing ADHD, people always seem to ask, "Just how many of them are there out there?" While it's impossible to know for sure, investigators have made some guesses based on observations and experience. Some estimates are a little far-fetched: educators in one survey back in the '50s indicated that 57% of boys and 42% of girls in their schools were overactive (Lapouse & Monk, 1958). Clearly, these figures are high, but they do serve to illustrate one point. Just as in "special education classes" (where boys usually outnumber the girls), there are far more males than females diagnosed with ADHD. In the literature we've read, boys seem to be 3 to 10 times more likely to be identified. In Ontario, Szatmari, Offord, and Boyle (1989) found the incidence of ADHD to be 9% in males and 3.3% in females. Hyperactive girls, then, may be part of a "silent minority" (Berry, Shaywitz, & Shaywitz, 1985). Thus, Amber finds herself in a double-whammy situation, for while ADHD boys tend to be misunderstood, ADHD girls are usually terribly misunderstood.

Investigators also disagree on the proportion of ADHD children in the general population. In Manitoba, we would likely say 2% (after all, we've arbitrarily identified 2% learning disabled, 2% behaviorally disruptive, 2% gifted/talented, 2% physically or mentally challenged, etc., etc. *ad infinitum*—we're down to 2% normal). Seriously, with the disintegration of family values, limited time (due to parents trying to earn enough to put bread on the table), neglect, latchkey children, and lack of discipline, a trend may be developing. Many educators feel there are more disruptive, "hyper" kids in school than there were a few years ago.

Depending on how cutoff points are selected, the figures in the literature vary from 1% to over 29% (Szatmari, Offord, & Boyle, 1989; Taylor, 1986; Weyandt, 2001). One study rating a large sample of school children (and using a criterion of 1.5 standard deviations above the mean) suggested that some 14% might be hyperactive (Trites, Dugas, Lynch, & Ferguson, 1979). When a more stringent criterion (of 2 standard deviations above the mean) is used, the incidence of ADHD tends to drop to somewhere in the 2% to 9% range. In the United States, the generally accepted prevalence rate is 3% to 5% (American Psychiatric Association, 1994). Even if the lower figures are the more accurate, the numbers are significant. For teachers, it means that they are likely to encounter overactive children in their classes on a regular basis. Since such youngsters can be terribly troublesome (and make it, at times, almost impossible to teach), it behooves educators to know how to deal with hyperactivity when it confronts them.

Identification

A lot of people have spent a lot of time worrying about how to identify the hyperactive child. Although there are different viewpoints, the consensus appears to be that observation is the best approach. We categorically concur. It seems logical to us that one-shot assessments are often unfair for these youngsters. Many hyperactive kids, because of their short concentration spans, don't do well in traditional testing situations. For one thing, they can't stick to task long enough to work to potential and, for another, they have often missed acquiring basic information due to their attentional problems.

Psychologists, pediatricians, and psychiatrists are frequently put in the position of having to make a diagnosis from a brief office visit—

another imperfect way of doing things. Some hyperactive kids can behave beautifully and pay attention well for short periods of time (particularly in novel situations), which may lead a doctor to think, mistakenly, that a little angel has crossed the threshold. In contrast, some generally well-behaved kids might act out badly in the same office setting, and perhaps be misdiagnosed. Also, relying on parental input alone isn't always enough; there are many misconceptions out there, and even a few parents who seem to need to have a sick (and labeled) child. We know many youngsters who, in our view, have been diagnosed inappropriately as ADHD, chiefly because the parents pushed for it.

Again, we would recommend taking a global, longitudinal approach to identification. Where possible, before a firm diagnosis of attention deficit is made, collaboration should take place among parents, relatives, significant others, educators, and medical personnel. We believe that, with classic attention-deficit/hyperactivity disorder (combined type), similar behavioral tendencies are on display at home, at school, and in the community. In other words, parents, teachers, and others will all notice the same type of behavior, and usually all will have difficulty coping with the child's overactive style. As indicated earlier, should a child be hyper at home, but not at school (or vice versa), another diagnosis should likely be considered.

It only makes sense to get input from many individuals when making a diagnosis of hyperactivity. Rather than relying on a short visit to the pediatrician, psychiatrist, or school psychologist, it is more reasonable to take a longitudinal look, and observe the child's behavior over time at home and at school. For an idea of what to look for, we would suggest turning to classic works in the area (Barkley, 1991, 1998; Conners & Wells, 1986; Goldstein & Goldstein, 1998).

On the WISC-III (Wechsler Intelligence Scale for Children-Third Edition), the most recent version of the IQ test most commonly run in the public schools, psychologists often look to the "freedom from distractibility" factor, an index made up of two specific subtests: Arithmetic (mental computation) and Digit Span (short-term auditory memory). However, although hyperactive students may well run into trouble with tasks requiring sustained concentration, there is little evidence to suggest that this particular index is helpful in detecting ADHD. In Barkley's (1998) opinion, IQ tests are best used for the purpose for which they were designed—they fall short when stretched in an unnatural attempt to identify attentional problems. The same goes for a large variety of neuropsychological tests.

A more recent test of intelligence, the Das-Naglieri CAS or Cognitive Assessment System (Naglieri & Das, 1997), may have more to offer in this regard. Nonetheless, while there are some early indications that ADHD children tend to perform poorly on CAS subtests measuring attention and planning (Paolitto, 1999), more thorough evaluation of this instrument is clearly necessary.

In recent years, CPTs (Continuous Performance Tests) such as Gordon's (1988) Diagnostic System, Conners' (1999b) Continuous Performance Test, and Greenberg's (1990) TOVA (Test of Variables of Attention) have grown in popularity. Basically, CPTs involve the presentation of stimuli—numbers or figures—via computer. The person being assessed is asked to press a button each time a target stimulus is presented and to refrain from so doing when non-target stimuli appear. Obviously, concentration is required. Although Goldstein and Goldstein (1998) have raised concerns about false positives (non-ADHDers being incorrectly flagged) and false negatives (ADHDers performing normally and being missed), there is a body of research that suggests CPTs can be useful in discriminating between individuals with and without ADHD, identifying subtypes of the disorder, and measuring effects of stimulants (Corkum & Siegel, 1993; Marks, Himelstein, Newcorn, & Halperin, 1999; Rapport, Tucker, DuPaul, Merlo, & Stoner, 1986). If used cautiously and wisely, continuous performance tests seem to have something to offer in the diagnosis of attentional problems.

One popular method used in identification of ADHD children is the rating scale approach. Of course, rating scales are not intended as definitive inventories to be used alone, but rather as guides for parents, teachers, and practitioners. They are only one piece of the assessment process (and should be used along with medical examinations, more formal testing, clinical interviews, and long-term evaluation and observation in real-life situations). By giving parents, teachers, and others a general appreciation for ADHD traits, rating scales, paradoxically, introduce some "objective subjectivity" into the assessment process.

Without doubt, the most widely used tools of this type in the schools are the Conners Rating Scales (Conners, 1997). Since, in some cases, parents and teachers have an opportunity to complete similar forms, different perspectives emerge of the child. It's possible to see where parents and teachers agree, where they disagree, and in what areas they might work together. A dual approach of this sort fosters partnerships, collaboration, and joint problem solving (which are critical elements in understanding and dealing effectively with the hyperactive child). Other scales focus on the ADHD adult (Conners, 1999a), and self-report instruments are also available.

In his work in the schools, the first author collaborated with a colleague to design two rating scales for use locally. The first, called the Short Subjective Hyperactivity Rating Index For Teachers, pulled together global descriptors from DSM-III and DSM-III-R (DSM-IV wasn't out at the time) in a parsimonious and to-the-point format. The facetious acronym, Short SHRIFT, describes what ADHD children often receive from certain teachers. The second, a more recent, comprehensive instrument called the Children's Activity Rating Scale, uses a five-point format with a neutral center. Unlike many other inventories, this scale avoids forcing choices in one direction, and balances negative and positive items in random fashion. More information about these two identification tools is available elsewhere (Stevens & McCluskey, 1998).

To reiterate, most professionals now believe that no one approach will do a decent job of accurately identifying ADHD. When considering the aforementioned alternatives, some school districts go so far as to insist upon "all of the above": they require student, teacher, and parental input, longitudinal observation, rating scales, psychological assessment with a variety of instruments (including continuous performance tests), and medical consultation before intervention can take place. Other jurisdictions, concerned about the time element and programming delays, choose what they consider to be the best predictors, and run with those. In most cases, though, it is standard practice today to use at least some combination of approaches in striving for accurate diagnosis of ADHD.

Causation (Why Her? And Why Us?)

A look at the literature dealing with etiology suggests that there seem to be multiple causes of attention deficit. There is much evidence to indicate that genetic influences and inheritance play a major role (Barkley, 1998). A variety of possible factors have been identified, including brain neurotransmitter deficiencies, neurotoxins, small lesions, unusual theta wave activity, frontal-lobe abnormalities, thyroid problems, premature birth, decreased cerebral blood flow, and underarousal of the central nervous system. ADHD has been linked to a gene that regulates the action of the neurotransmitter dopamine; various hypotheses cite selective dopamine depletion and dysfunction in the orbital-limbic pathways of the frontal area of the brain as a major cause of the condition (Barkley, 1998). Along with dopamine, noradrenalin and serotonin neurons also appear to be involved in dysfunction of the attentional system (Goldstein & Goldstein, 1998).

Not everyone subscribes to the view that ADHD is a medical condition. On the contrary, many investigators assert that ADHD has been socially constructed, and that research suggesting it is a biological disorder is unproven and flawed (Breggin, 1998; DeGrandpre, 1999; Diller, 1998; Nylund, 2000; Stein, 1999).

In the future, researchers may well be able to point with more confidence to precise genetic causes of ADHD. For now, though, there is a great deal of uncertainty; much more work remains to be done. To further complicate matters, some prescription drugs can cause overactivity (e.g., decongestant, anti-asthmatic, and anti-epileptic medication), and some parents and physicians believe that food additives (preservatives, coloring, etc.) and refined sugars (in candy, primarily) also contribute. The literature here is equivocal at best (cf. Barkley, 1998; Goldstein & Goldstein, 1998), but these explanations remain popular among the general public. It goes without saying that many environmental and psychoeducational variables are frequently involved in causing or increasing the severity of attentional deficits and overactive behavior.

As far as we're concerned, causation isn't the major issue; we've always known that Amber was a few synapses short a transmission. We've got what we've got, and we have to deal with concrete symptoms, not ethereal theorizing.

Also, although we see the causes of hyperactivity as being both genetic and environmental, we resist being drawn into the age-old heredity-environment debate. We think it's rather pointless to argue back and forth about which is "the cause"—it's always both (McCluskey & Walker, 1986). Heredity and environment are inextricably interwoven in human development, for even in the womb you can't have one without the other. As Roberts (1967) noted, humans—at any point in the life cycle—are what they are because of their hereditary constitution and the nature of the environment in which they have lived. The two factors are inseparable.

As educators and parents, though, we much prefer to take an environmentalist position. Things are evolving rapidly on the scientific front, but for the moment there is not much most of us can do about heredity—genes are genes. Regardless of what we have to work with at the start, however, we can intervene and enrich a child's environment in many ways. Most parents and teachers can't change nature, but we can, and should, modify and improve environmental conditions at home and at school as much as possible.

When all is said and done, we are forced to ask ourselves, "Why agonize over the whys?" Whatever the reason, Amber is unusual, and she is clearly hyperactive. Knowing something about the disorder is helpful, but focusing too much on etiology and theory can sometimes inhibit action. Whatever the cause, parents and teachers are the ones placed in the position of having to deal with the problem. While we should strive for understanding, we must not stop there—we also need to do something concrete and meaningful to make the lives of ADHDers more enjoyable, productive, and rewarding.

Primary Characteristics

Although different investigators naturally take different tacks, a few primary characteristics of hyperactivity are noted over and over again in the literature. Such primary symptoms are direct and highly visible—main ingredients to look for in identifying ADHD. Our plan is to discuss first some of the primary characteristics that apply to Amber and other "hyper" individuals. At this preliminary stage, we'll take a very broad, generic view. In the next chapter, we'll present specific real-life, "Amberian" examples to highlight each of these traits (and the problems they cause). Speaking generally, then, the following symptoms are typical of many classically hyperactive children:

Overactivity

ADHD children tend to have difficulty remaining still or staying seated—at home and at school. If asked to sit and pay attention, they have trouble restraining themselves and often fidget in "wormy-squirmy" fashion. In DSM-IV, it is stated—quite accurately—that hyperactive children are constantly "on the go" as if "driven by a motor".

At home, overactive youngsters run about or climb all over the place, and they frequently move excessively even during sleep. In school, teachers often report, in despair, that hyperactive kids simply cannot sit still. Such children typically wiggle their legs or arms, fiddle with objects, or move their bodies as if they just have to get up. Many try to leave their seats whenever possible. Because of their tendency toward perpetual motion, hyperactive students spend much of their time pestering and annoying other children in class.

Teachers know the hyper kids—they're the ones who can't stay seated, who fidget all day long, and who make the class a living hell. To identify ADHD informally, simply look at the child's clothes and shoes—they wear out much faster than normal. (On top of everything else, hyperactive kids are expensive.) Also, again by way of informal diagnosis, watch for the kids who have to check out the washroom 30 or 40 times a day—it gives them a chance to get out and about. Although people often think there is something physically wrong with these youngsters, they usually just need to move. In other words, they have to go even when they don't have to go. Along the same lines, one can often pick out the overactive kids by their pencils, which are usually reduced to tiny, shrunken stubs. Since getting up to sharpen one's pencil is socially acceptable, these kids do it frequently. When they are confined to their seats for longer than they can possibly stand (it doesn't have to be very long), this activity provides a way of escape. However, such constant running to the pencil sharpener, to the washroom, or to visit neighbors can prove extremely disruptive—these kids are tough to manage in the classroom.

Inattention

Commonly, hyperactive children fail to finish things that they start. Often such children don't seem to listen, and they appear to have incredible difficulty sustaining attention (Seidel & Joschko, 1990) or staying on task for more than a few minutes at a time. As a result, it's almost inevitable that they cannot focus on schoolwork or any other task requiring intense concentration. This short attention span shows up not only in school or work-related activities, but at play as well. ADHDers usually do not play well alone, but rather have a need to be running about, poking, or otherwise disturbing playmates.

Even when they manage to hold their bodies still, the minds of hyperactive children have a tendency to wander. While motor restlessness is usually present, mental restlessness or "underfocusing" can be a problem, even during the rare calm moments. The failure of these kids to maintain their concentration often causes them to make bad decisions, to fail to follow through with tasks or chores, and generally to get into trouble. With many cases of ADHD, the problem is not only motoric overactivity, but also lack of concentration when at rest (Kinsbourne & Swanson, 1978). Selective focusing is evident now and again (particularly in novel settings or with stimulating activities), but the general trend is toward daydreaming and mental restlessness.

Distractibility

Along the same lines, hyperactive children often fail to finish tasks, largely because they are so easily distracted from the work at hand. While they may be intensely interested in something (and focus on it for a brief time), they tend to fly away the moment something else captures their attention. To illustrate, such children may be totally engrossed in a television show, but the moment a new idea strikes them they head off helter-skelter in a completely different direction (forgetting what they were doing in the first place). A few minutes later, they may be off again to something else. It appears that these hyperactive children are not only easily distracted, but that they need and "welcome" distraction. It's part of who they are.

In our experience, ADHD children can, on occasion, stick with certain tasks. Some, for example, seem able to concentrate reasonably well on video and computer games. For the most part, though, hyperactive children rarely focus on one activity for more than four or five minutes at a time (and often end up jumping wildly from game to game even on computer—they're at the machine, but not able to focus on just one thing). This distractibility makes them very difficult to manage in the classroom, where they are faced with, and usually resist, limit-setting. Because they cannot concentrate on a single activity for any length of time (tending instead to switch back and forth from task to task), attention deficit children frequently end up learning a great deal of irrelevant material, while missing much of what is being taught. Thus, while these youngsters may learn certain things in school, it is usually not what they were expected to learn.

Impulsivity

Overactive children often act quickly, without thinking. They lack impulse control, in that they want what they want when they want it. Because of this trait, ADHDers naturally have trouble following rules or waiting their turn. Such children make bad decisions, often by moving when "it's wise to be still" (Kinsbourne & Swanson, 1978). They may run into the street without looking, dive into swimming pools without checking the depth of the water (or even without knowing how to swim), ride bicycles without caution, and react and talk without thinking things through. Melmed (2001) has remarked that ADHD kids exhibit defective hindsight (they don't seem to learn from experience), defective forethought (they don't plan ahead efficiently), and an unrealistic, diminished sense of time (they don't know how long things take).

Not unexpectedly given their propensity for acting so impulsively, hyperactive youngsters tend to get into accidents. This is not to say that all overactive kids are physically accident-prone by any means; many are agile, active, and known for their ability to escape from dicey situations. Sometimes, though, their reputation for invulnerability is exaggerated; several of these kids escape a lot precisely because they get into so many scrapes. In many instances, however, it eventually catches up with them, and physical injury does result. Since many of these youngsters run headlong into unfamiliar situations, it is not surprising that hospital records show that ADHD children do, in fact, end up paying more than their share of visits for repairs (for broken bones, eye injuries, and such).

Further, while some active children may be extremely agile, others are not. A case in point is a little guy who attended a school we served some years back. He was a good-natured child and talented in many respects. As well, though, he tended to lose concentration and be rather "klutzy". We realized just how much at risk this boy was the day we saw him approach a bright area in the school, where sunlight was pouring in through the Venetian blinds. Without a word of a lie, this unfortunate student consistently tripped over the beams of light shining on the floor.

Excitability

ADHD children typically have what might be termed low frustration tolerance or, to put it more colloquially, "short fuses". Although they want to have playmates, they are often upset or "set off" by them. Hyper kids are easily excited: they get into kerfuffles with other children, and, when taken to task by parents or teachers, tend to be extremely emotional and in a mad rush to explain their side of the story. While hyperactivity does not necessarily manifest itself in malevolent or malicious ways, sometimes ADHD individuals do exhibit oppositional defiant disorder, where highly recalcitrant behavior, verbal arguments, and even physical set-tos are the order of the day.

Excitability can cause all sorts of problems for hyperactive children. We've noticed that many ADHD kids are extremely apologetic: they get into trouble, feel bad about it, apologize nonstop, and promise sincerely to do better next time around. But they can't, and they don't. Despite a genuine desire to be good and to improve, they are unable to restrain themselves or settle down. Then, of course, parents and teachers— feeling betrayed and lied to—get extremely upset, and the whole situation escalates (leading to ultimatums, threats, and tension).

Disorganization

According to DSM-IV, children with attention-deficit/hyperactivity disorder often "have difficulty organizing tasks and activities". Not surprisingly, considering their impulsivity and excitability, overactive youngsters typically mismanage work and play. And their hyper disorganization can affect the lives of others. Our daughter's penchant for moving furniture about has caused her mother to ask in desperation, "Amber, where's my sofa?" (McCluskey, McCluskey, McCluskey, & McCluskey, in press). One might make a case for disorganization being a secondary characteristic, but to educators, at least, it appears very dominant and primary. At school, overactive, inattentive kids are at a great disadvantage because they can't keep themselves or their belongings straight. ADHD students require ongoing and intensive supervision—they are unable to stay on track without it. Organizational issues become a real concern both at home and at school, with the kids continually mislaying or losing supplies, books, homework, day planners, clothes, and even treasured possessions. Parents of hyperactive children can usually be found near the school's lost-and-found bin—they virtually live there.

Secondary Characteristics

A number of writers have also identified a variety of secondary symptoms or characteristics associated with hyperactivity. While they may not be the central ingredients or descriptors of the disorder, these traits are frequently found as secondary factors or offshoots of the primary problems. To state it somewhat differently, the secondary characteristics can grow out of the primary features of ADHD—one thing (primary symptoms) leads to another (secondary issues). Secondary behaviors are sometimes more remediable—they can often be addressed effectively by examining and restructuring social situations, philosophies, and educational approaches. Again, although there is considerable overlap (and no real need, from our perspective, to make fine distinctions), the following secondary characteristics have hit home for us:

Peer Relationship Problems

Many overactive children are not only at risk physically, but they are socially accident-prone as well. Due to their lack of impulse control, they tend to do and say the wrong things over and over again. Their impulsive behavior and resulting errors of judgment often cause attention deficit children to be unpopular with their peer group and classmates. Naturally, all children, at times, engage in hyper-like behavior. But there is a difference in degree: ADHD kids switch erratically from activity to activity, fidget, and have a great deal of difficulty sticking to a task or completing work at any time. The overactivity and impulsivity are, in a way, the essence of their being.

Because of their full-speed-ahead style, ADHD youngsters are frequently not sensitive to the needs of others. They can't slow down long enough to think about their behavior and its effects, so they often miss cues, misread social situations, and get into trouble. Essentially, they tend to take a bossy, "play-it-my-way-or-not-at-all" approach (Wender, 1987).

Most children's actions are, at least much of the time, planned in advance and purposeful to some extent. In contrast, hyperactive kids simply react—rapidly and unpredictably. They're terminally inquisitive, as it were: they see something they want, grab at it impulsively, and then become offended and hurt when others are upset with them. It's self-evident that such volatile and disruptive behavior patterns will result in conflict with peers, parents, and teachers—ADHD kids can quickly become unpopular in a wide variety of settings. And since they fail to pick up on social cues or learn from consequences, they stay unpopular. This poor social judgment is particularly noticeable in adolescence, when most of the other young people have developed their communication skills and become more "clued in" than their ADHD counterparts (such as Amber).

It is not unusual to find that hyperactive children have a problem forming interpersonal relationships. These youngsters often desperately want friends, but don't know how to find or keep them. Sometimes, they will do almost anything to make friends, to the point of trying to "buy" them with candies, money, or whatnot. This technique may work for a while, but, with their lack of restraint, attention deficit children usually end up disturbing and offending others after a short period of time. Since they can't hold themselves back, ADHDers tend not to be understanding or empathic—their "friendships" usually don't last all that long. The result is tremendous inconsistency and bouncing, at high speed, from one revolving friendship to another. It is rather sad to see such kids desperately seeking friends, only to "turn off" any they may find.

From a parental point of view, it is worrisome when, in a vain quest for companionship, ADHD children try to bond with "anybody". Because they need friends so badly, they often gravitate toward, and cling to, "bad actors". Anyone, no matter how "undesirable", will do, if only they will play with them and give them the time of day. In adolescence, ADHD teens may seek out the company of younger children who pose less of a threat to them (Weiner, 1982).

For anyone who works with attention deficit children, the term "socially accident-prone" makes a great deal of sense. It is clear that youngsters who have trouble with complex rules and games are likely to run afoul of others. During a game of baseball during recess, for example, most children have the self-control to wait, if necessary, for three balls and two strikes—hyperactive kids may not. As a consequence, these children benefit from intensive playground supervision to help them handle social situations. This is particularly true when complex rules and structured games, rather than free play, are involved.

The problem with play is a real issue, especially since many parents and educators (with the best will in the world) mistakenly encourage hyperactive children to run and play with others to "burn off energy". It really isn't that simple. In some cases, the burning-off-energy theory works, but in other instances it may simply be setting ADHD kids up for failure. If left unchecked, their impulsivity will interfere markedly with the activities of other youngsters and be counterproductive to relationship building. Active supervision is often required.

Another intriguing characteristic is the tendency for hyperactive children to lie. Of course, parents and teachers are the first to notice that ADHD kids frequently bend the truth a long way. This sort of lying can be damaging, for often stories or comments made by hyperactive children are ill-conceived, obviously false, and easy to hold up to ridicule. Lying truly is a major characteristic of ADHD (Ingersoll, 1988), and it can be particularly debilitating in a social sense. Even worse, impulsive stealing can occur, which also causes all kinds of problems at home, at school, or in the community.

It is important to realize that lying is not a symptom of a vicious or evil personality, but rather part and parcel of overactive children's inability to control their behavior. They move their mouths as carelessly as their bodies. For most of us, if we are about to utter a lie, we often reflect, consider the moral implications, and keep quiet. Or less nobly, but perhaps more realistically, we realize the lie is not a good one, and hold back until we can think of a more cogent untruth. Lacking this ability to restrain themselves, ADHD children exhibit the unfortunate inclination to blurt out the first thing that comes to mind, no matter how inane. Such patently ridiculous falsehoods can be very destructive in social situations, and interfere with bonding or forming relationships with peers. Shrewder (though not necessarily nicer) children often start scapegoating and, with their problem behavior, ADHD kids are remarkably easy targets.

Learning Problems

Since ADHD children have difficulty focusing, paying attention, and even staying at their desks, it is not surprising to find that they typically have trouble in school. This is not to say that they are slow learners by any means, but their inability to stay on task interferes markedly with the acquisition of basic skills. Usually, hyperactive children are not all that interested in reading, for they prefer a more hands-on, touchy-feely, learning-by-doing approach. Nonetheless, for many, reading isn't an impossible task—several attention deficit children do acquire at least reasonable reading skills. While they may well lag noticeably behind their classmates, reading usually comes along to some extent. To be more precise, although hyper youngsters tend not to be facile readers, reading still may be a relative strength, in that they're less behind here than in other areas (assuming there are no specific learning disabilities).

For many of the ADHDers we've encountered, academic deficits are most pronounced in subjects that require ongoing concentration and work. For example, learning to write well takes quite an effort, what with organizing, outlining, preparing an initial draft, editing, polishing, and so on. Clearly, this process demands concentration that hyperactive children lack. Related problems surface in math as well, where the same kind of consistency and work ethic are needed. Attention deficit children often simply can't manage it. It's important to recognize that, in their way, hyperactive children can be extremely bright and talented. Of late, some investigators have pointed to a possible link between ADHD and creativity (Cramond, 1994; Cramond, Gollmar, & Calic, 1994; Hartmann, 1997). However, despite possible strengths in the oral/verbal domain, theater, and movement activities (such as dance or sports), hyperactive children and school usually don't mix—these kids just don't have the attention span. According to some, the learning problems typically become severe enough that 60%–70% of hyperactive youngsters are retained at least once in school (Schwartz & Johnson, 1987; Weiner, 1982). Indeed, some contend that ADHD children are 2 to 3 times more likely than other students to be retained at least once during their elementary years (Greenberg & Horn, 1991).

To further exacerbate the situation, frustration due to these learning problems can lead to bruised self-concept, alienation, and defiant conduct. It has been suggested that a large proportion of attention deficit students fail to finish high school, and that very few pursue post-secondary education (Fischer, Barkley, Edelbrock, & Smallish, 1990; Weiss, Hechtman, Milroy, & Perlman, 1985).

Again, while many hyperactive students possess adequate enough cognitive potential, they tend to have learning problems simply because they cannot settle down long enough to absorb material. To complicate matters still further, it has been observed that learning disability (LD) and hyperactivity frequently go hand in hand (Cantwell & Baker, 1991; Dykman & Ackerman, 1991; Greenberg & Horn, 1991; Ingersoll, 1988; Silver, 1990). Some writers feel the number of hyperactive children with learning disabilities is extremely high—in the 60%–80% range (Safer & Allen, 1976). Others offer a more moderate, yet still highly significant estimate of 20% (Silver, 1992).

Other researchers disagree, or are at least more doubtful about the relationship between LD and ADHD (Murphy & Hicks-Stewart, 1991). Certainly, neither attention deficit nor learning disability are cut-and-dried disorders; there's a lot going on in both that we don't yet understand. It is hard to say whether learning problems of particular students are due to short attention span, underachievement, or learning disabilities—a multiplicity of factors are usually involved. There are differing degrees of hyperactivity, and clearly many variations on the original theme. Similarly, disabilities can be classic and profound or softer and less pervasive. To us, the only way to take a proper look at attention deficit, learning problems, and disability is on an individual basis. We must treat each child as a unique entity, not a syndrome, and proceed in an unbiased way (without having any preconceived notions). When issues are so complex, there is a need for caution—it is a mistake to take a dogmatic approach because of what we think we know. In light of the literature, we must acknowledge, in some cases, the possibility of a link between attention deficit and disability. On the other hand, we don't want to force or predetermine a diagnosis, or see things that aren't there.

We'd like to reemphasize the point that ADHDers may be extremely bright, in their odd, off-the-wall fashion. One little nipper we've known, a decidedly hyperactive youngster in grade 2, gave us a memorable example of "smarts", combined with lack of knowledge. Actually, when assessing this lad many years ago, we were doing all the things good testers shouldn't do. Because of time pressures, we were rushed; there were just too many kids to see. Despite our haste, it was impossible to get this little guy to hurry. Although he didn't know many of the answers, he would creatively try to figure things out. One question on the old WISC-R (Wechsler Intelligence Scale for Children-Revised)—the instrument we administered at the time—asks, "What does the stomach do?" We knew full well that the kid didn't understand the digestive process or have an answer, yet, when we tried to move on, he yelled out: "Hold it, I'm thinking!" He couldn't come up with anything, so we tried to move on once more. Again, the boy bellowed: "Wait, I'm still thinking!" We finally had to say: "Look, we've got to get moving. If you have an answer, give it to us. What does the stomach do?" At that point, in desperation, he blurted out: "If we didn't have stomachs, our heads would be on our bums." No, he didn't understand the digestive process, but he certainly was thinking.

A little later in the session, this youngster came up with another answer that we found quite startling. On the Vocabulary subtest, he was asked to define words. This boy was moving along quite famously when, all of a sudden—just after we had presented the word *donkey*—we lost him: he had simply drifted off into his own little world. In an effort to recapture his attention, one of us repeated the word, with an inflection indicating that a response was called for (*don-key* ...). Amazingly, this young man, recalled from his reverie, looked up abruptly and answered "Ho-tay". After questioning, we discovered that he definitely meant Don Quixote. He knew all about Cervantes, *Man of La Mancha*, and tilting at windmills. His objective test results weren't good, but his problem was distractibility, not inability.

Since it arises so often, it's probably wise to think about reading disability, or what is termed *dyslexia*, a little more carefully. In the classic sense, learning disabled individuals have average or above average potential in most respects, but a "fatal flaw" in reading or some other area. For example, try as they might, some dyslexics can't grasp the intricacies of sound-symbol association or word attack. Students with this problem struggle with decoding or sounding out unfamiliar material. While such youngsters may be able to learn their consonant and vowel sounds, they have trouble pulling things together or blending effectively. Thus, they are often put in the unfortunate position of having to read almost entirely by sight alone (and make guesses from only first consonants or partial configurations). They just can't sound things out. One grade 4 boy we tested had this problem, but he was "quick as a whip" in making logical inferences. Although he used contextual cues effectively, he didn't have the word attack skills to proceed very far. As a result, he guessed logically, but incorrectly, on the basis of initial consonants alone. To illustrate, when faced with the passage on the PIAT (Peabody Individual Achievement Test), "Mother is cutting pretty flowers," he responded with "Mother is cooking perogies fast." From his perspective, things made sense, but the word attack deficiencies were clearly getting very much in the way of reading and overall comprehension.

Youngsters reading by sight alone tend to plateau at the grade 4 or 5 level, largely because there is a limit to the number of words they can memorize. And even when disabled readers manage to score higher on formal tests, they are often not reading in a natural or fluid fashion. That is, their performance says more about their compensatory strategies and intellect than it does about reading per se.

Reluctant or disabled readers also frequently look at words in isolation rather than in context, stumble over "small" words (such as *and*, *the*, *a*, and *but*) that should be automatic, but aren't, insert or delete material inappropriately, and generally proceed in a slow, laborious manner. Their reading tends to be painfully cumbersome since they lack flow and rhythm, and they usually don't care for it much at all. Such distaste isn't surprising; most of us don't enjoy or spend much time on activities we're not good at. Reversals are another common problem. Specifically, reading disabled students sometimes have difficulty distinguishing between *b*/*d*, *p*/*q*, *was* and *saw*, *drop* and *prod*, *pun* and *bun*, and so on. By the way, it is a mistake to panic about reversals too early, for it is very common for youngsters to reverse material before form constancy is established. However, if the reversals continue into the late primary grades and beyond, there could be cause for concern.

Familial Problems

With all their irregular and unpredictable behavioral tendencies, overactive children can be a sore trial at home—they put tremendous pressure on parents (Barkley, 1989, 2000; Weiner, 1982). A great deal has been written about the strain that ADHD children place on caregivers (Moghadam, 1988; Taylor, 1980; Wender, 1987).

Attention deficit children, while they may be extremely well-meaning and lovable, unintentionally catalyze family conflict. Parents may find themselves at a loss, disagree about how to handle certain situations, and end up arguing or taking different directions. If parents don't communicate and work closely with each other, hyperactive children can cause all sorts of chaos and instability. In fact, it wouldn't surprise us to find that ADHDers are one of the major causes of divorce in North America.

Low Self-Concept

Parents, teachers, and others usually find hyper kids difficult and frustrating to deal with, and these frustrations show. And because the youngsters don't understand and can't control their behaviors, the problems and negative reactions typically build.

Since hyperactive children are always in so much trouble and blamed, often quite rightly, for problems with siblings at home and peers at school, they have little opportunity to see themselves in a positive light. Many ADHD youngsters get a continual dose of criticism from all sides, to the point where, over time, they begin to take a totally negative view of themselves and their actions.

It is sad to see children who, because they incur everyone's wrath, have no place to turn for safety and support. Parents and teachers have good intentions of helping ADHD youngsters (by laying down rules and structure), but sometimes these intentions result in an endless, unbroken barrage of anger and impatient nagging, and a concomitant assault on self-concept. One proverb goes, "The nail that stands the tallest gets the hammer." All too often, ADHDers—who stand out for negative, not positive reasons —are indeed "hammered" unmercifully, and they can't adjust or turn over a new leaf. It is easy to see how children "failing" in academics, peer relationships, and other social interactions might become depressed and feel worthless. To make matters worse, it doesn't take long for the overactive child to get a "bad reputation" at school and in the community. In a once-popular rap song, a mother tells her child, "You're only 16, you don't have a rep yet." Sadly, this is not true for many hyperactive children, who end up being labeled and written off shortly after they enter school.

The matter of self-image has long been of concern (Ingersoll, 1988; Wender, 1987); it's disturbing to hear countless hyperactive children echo the same refrain, "Nobody likes me!" Even though such youngsters don't intend to be "bad", it often ends up that way, they're treated that way, and they begin to view themselves that way. Another issue is comorbidity, where—for many sufferers—ADHD coexists not only with learning disability, but with conduct, mood, sleep, eating, tic/movement, and other disorders as well (Children and Adults with Attention Deficit Disorders, 1996; Fisher & Beckley, 1998; Melmed, 2001; Robin, 1998). Substance abuse is also often found in the mix. One of the greatest challenges with ADHD is to address the problems while maintaining and building self-concept.

Chapter 3

AMBER'S HYPERACTIVE JOURNEY

Once more, it's important to stress that we don't view either the primary or secondary characteristics as being hard-and-fast "laws"—we see them simply as loose guidelines to help us conceptualize hyperactivity as a process. Naturally, these traits are not mutually exclusive; there's all sorts of intertwining and overlap. Still, with this schema in place, it is possible to move ahead cautiously in an attempt to describe and understand Amber's behavior. We'll now revisit our six primary and four secondary characteristics of hyperactivity, fitting Amber's intriguing, sometimes bizarre antics into each. This is precisely where we hope the book will start to come alive, and where the reader will begin to grasp the enormous impact hyperactivity has on parents, teachers, and the child. We now get into "feeling" hyperactivity, rather than merely knowing about it. From this point on, we expect plenty of empathy and sympathy.

Although we don't intend to do it in a highly structured fashion, generally—for each characteristic or symptom—we will work through Amber's behavior patterns more or less in chronological order, from her younger to her older years. Thus, we will endeavor to paint a picture of a growing and maturing Amber (we use the word "maturing" very loosely).

Overactivity

The term "wormy-squirmy" describes Amber to a tee. Right from birth, there was no downtime in parenting her; she was always "on the move". As an infant, Amber didn't seem to need all that much sleep, and she spent most of her time crying and disrupting the household. There was very little rest, night or day, for anyone in the vicinity. It is no fun for parents to share their bed with a hyper child. Whenever Amber crawled under the covers with us, she would twist, turn, kick in her sleep, worm around, and generally make it impossible for us to get a moment's shut eye—talk about nonrelaxing! She had to snuggle in between the two of us, so she could thrash wildly and annoy each equally. Also, Amber would always kick off the blankets, so it was impossible to keep warm. We had to use the cats!

Even when Amber was in her own bedroom, there was still no rest for us parents. Her rocking (back and forth in synch) was often audible, and we could hear strains of "Old MacDonald" emanating from her room virtually any time during the night. On a more distressing note, Amber also suffered from night terrors for a couple of years. When she finally did get to sleep, she often had terrible dreams (which were incredibly difficult to wake her from). It was as if she were making up for lost sleeping time every now and again, to the point where she couldn't rouse herself or escape from the nightmares. Luckily, that phase soon passed. The basic trend, however, continued: Amber was abnormally active, getting into every conceivable thing, all day long. And she would sleep very little at day's end. Unless you've been there as a parent, it's very hard to understand how draining this routine can be.

George Mager, an educational psychologist who taught some years ago at McGill University in Montreal, has a lot to say concerning sleep disturbance and hyperactivity. He knows of what he speaks, for Mager himself has been diagnosed with attention deficit. In some of his fascinating presentations, Mager has remarked that he too has difficulty sleeping at night. In fact, his pattern is to stay up past midnight, power nap for a couple of hours, wake up, put coffee on, and work on lectures for a spell. Then he returns to bed for an additional hour or two, before rising for the day. Obviously, he sleeps very little. Apparently, Mager has been informed by doctors that this behavior might eventually become life-threatening; his sleeping time is that far below average. However, Mager thinks not—he feels he is simply wired up to operate this way. And as he notes, even if he does die early, in the meantime he will have "lived four lifetimes!"

Getting back to Amber, imagine how difficult it is to manage a youngster who rarely sleeps for several hours in succession, but instead power naps for brief (never consecutive) intervals. Because Mom, on occasion, needed a bit of sleep of her own, Amber—as an infant— often found herself in a portable swing (which, in that premotorized era, was tied to the arm of Mom's rocking chair). Even when Mom dozed off, rocking would continue, and Amber could receive her necessary movement and stimulation. When placed in her crib, Amber tossed, thrashed, and bounced, to the point where she would literally rock her crib across the room.

As a young child, Amber continued to have difficulty staying in her room and falling asleep. It was amazing the trouble she could generate after her "official bedtime". One day, after jumping into bed, she described herself innocently, but accurately, as "Snug as a bugger in a rug!" In her late preschool and early primary grade years, we developed other techniques to calm Amber down and help her sleep. When she curled up in bed, she loved for us to bend over and flutter our eyelashes against her cheek as a sign of affection. Amber looked forward to these eyelash rubs with warm anticipation. Somehow, that action was soothing for her. Picking up the term from popular folklore, she called the flutters "butterfly kisses".

From the beginning, Amber got into all sorts of trouble. It was necessary to supervise her virtually every second. For example, it was impossible to turn one's back while bathing Amber; if left to her own devices for even a moment, she would be climbing on the sink, leaping to the curtain rod, and attempting to hang upside down by her knees.

The kitchen was also a dangerous place, due to Amber's tendency to scramble up the inside of the fridge door like a fly and get into the cupboards overhead. When anyone asked, "Amber, how did you get up there?", her response was always, "It's easy." The possibilities for disaster were legion. In games like hide-and-seek, for example, Amber would do ill-judged things such as conceal herself in the oven! If we had ever relaxed our vigilance (by preheating without looking), we might well have ended up with cooked Amber.

AMBER IS BEING VERY QUIET SOMEWHERE.
SHE AND CHRIS ARE PLAYING HIDE AND SEEK.   W.S.

In an attempt to police Amber's behavior, we developed several techniques that frequently ended up causing us more aggravation than not. It was several years after Amber's birth, for example, before Mom could go to the washroom without leaving the door open—she always had to be on the alert. And Amber could not be allowed to leave home without supervision; that would have been absolutely disastrous. As a consequence, much of her independent play had to take place in the yard, under someone's watchful gaze. It was clearly impossible to leave Amber alone with children her own age. We made that mistake once or twice.

We recall one episode where Amber's Auntie Liv, who was baby-sitting at the time, asked Chris and his cousin Devron (who is the same age) to keep an eye on Amber in the backyard. Understandably enough, they found her impossible to manage. The first time she poked her head out to check, Liv found that the two young supervisors had handled the situation the only way they could. Chris and Dev were playing happily in the sandbox, but Amber was tied to the swing bar. So much for early years babysitting by the boys.

Once Amber hit the public school system, all hell broke loose—it was Hiroshima revisited. After her first few days in kindergarten, we were told that Amber was not ready for school. The teacher asked, in wild panic, "Don't you think you should keep her home?" That's a fine start, having a daughter who is virtually expelled from kindergarten. When we

LET'S GO! SHE'LL BE LOOSE IN FIVE MINUTES!

resisted this notion, a social worker was sent out to discover what form of abuse we were inflicting on this poor child (not realizing it was quite the opposite). In probing for information, the worker asked, "Do you love her?" Mom's response: "Of course I love her. Look at her. Would I have kept her if I didn't?"

In the community, it was no better. Because of her disruptive behavior, Amber was removed from swimming, kicked out of gymnastics, and asked to leave Brownies. With dance lessons, they offered to buy back her shoes if only we would take her out! In short, it was one disaster after another and Amber never fared well in any setting. Her overactivity definitely put affection to the test. One day in McDonald's, she was so rambunctious, running hither and yon at will, that mother, aunt, and grandma all tried to pin her down for a much needed swat on the behind. But they couldn't catch her—Amber was under tables, behind counters, and on the run throughout the entire place.

Back at school, there were more forewarnings of problems to come. Surviving various trials and tribulations, Amber stayed in kindergarten, and that year the teacher continued a tradition of helping the kids produce meaningful Mother's Day gifts—plaster imprints of their own hands. We felt this was a neat sort of present, and still treasure Chris's clear, firm little hand print from the previous year. When Amber, in her turn, had her "imprinting", the result was far different. She couldn't stay still during the sitting, what with her wiggling and squirming about, and her hand print was blurred, ill-defined, and just plain messy. We treasure her effort in this regard, too, but the prints are certainly different. One glance at our wall (where these mementos are hung) immediately reveals the difference between the two children.

The problems continued unabated through the primary grades. Our grade 1 parent interview was highly traumatic; her teacher cried! While some of Amber's behaviors were simply annoying, others were dangerous and actually life threatening. When we moved the next year from the big city to a smaller community, Amber, of course, went to a brand new school. The staff, who in their heart of hearts may have been less than delighted, were wonderful. We had a great deal of confidence in her teachers, and felt that Amber would get all kinds of attention and support in class and in the building. Knowing Amber, however, we were sure she was going to encounter some difficulties, especially on the playground. Therefore, on the first day of school, we decided to sneak away to see if we could keep an eye out for her during recess. Just as we were walking out of the office, the phone rang, which delayed us just a bit—we got to the school a minute or two after recess had begun. Scanning the playground quickly, we found her grade 2 class, but Amber was already missing in action. When we finally spotted her, she was naturally in the worst of all possible places. To our consternation, she had scurried up the hydro pole and was poised to begin moving along the electrical wires hand-over-hand. Trying to be calm, we called out, in positive tones, "Amber, we'd like to talk to you. Can you come down please?" We screamed out the riot act the moment she hit the ground! When we say we're amazed that Amber has made it through childhood and adolescence, we're only being partly facetious. There were plenty of scares along the way!

It didn't take extraordinary perspicacity to realize that something out of the common way was going on with this girl; she was different and demanding at home and at school. Naturally, we clamped down hard on the disruptive and life-threatening behavior, but it took a lot of clamping—Amber was the most disruptive of the disruptive. Even with good intentions, she could never contain or restrain herself.

As she grew, Amber's ADHD shifted and changed form, but it didn't go away. Although it lay dormant for short spells, it was more or less always there, waiting to burst forth. By the intermediate and junior high grades, some new patterns began to emerge at home. For one, when Amber went (or was sent) to her room, she would constantly clean and rearrange her furniture, moving everything about from one spot to another. Even now, she does minor furniture revisions almost daily, and not many weeks go by without her totally redoing several rooms in her house. By the way, in answer to the question "Amber, where's my sofa?" mentioned earlier: it was in the garage!

In high school, studying, especially initially, was almost impossible for Amber. She'd walk back and forth, pace, lean against the counter, jump up on it, swing her legs back and forth, recite material, and talk to herself incessantly. It's easy to see why she couldn't get a lot done in a formal class environment. Amber still looks for every excuse to move or grab at things: she loves to organize and sort objects, play with stickers or buttons, stuff her pockets full of candies, and move everything from here to there and back again. When shopping, she has to touch each item she sees; there is never a restful, tranquil moment in a store.

Even though Amber was retained in grade 6 (her teachers felt, accurately, that she was not ready for junior high either academically or socially), it still took a four-year plan to get her through high school. As a young adult, Amber improved, but her studying had to be done in very short intervals. Any long doses of concentration were rather overwhelming. Even when we forced her to "Sit still and study!", we saw the "mental hyperactivity". We watched Amber sitting, trying to focus on her books, and saw her thoughts drift away. Quite literally, she was mentally all revved up with no place to go. Often, this mental hyperactivity found expression through her "motor mouth syndrome", where she talked nonstop and leaped wildly from topic to topic.

It is still amazing to hear Amber speak and shift gears in her rapid-fire fashion. Her thoughts and words are fleeting, scattered, and "spinny"; just listening to her bouncy discourse wears you out.

Inattention

Partly due to her restlessness, Amber is forever drifting off-task; she never seems to pay attention. Interestingly, she can't even listen to herself for long; she jumps endlessly from subject to subject. In her preschool years, Amber's inattentive style was bothersome, but family members bore the full brunt of it. At school, though, the ramifications of her behavior became more widespread—she interfered with the learning of others. She didn't mean to be mean, but she really was a disruptive influence.

One thing that struck us was that Amber didn't even know how to play on her own. Most parents have various crosses to bear, but not many have to teach their children how to play! When she was in grade 2, we bought Amber what seemed like the entire Barbie Doll ensemble, complete with cars, houses, and other accessories. Amber had it all when it came to Barbie, but so what? She didn't know what to do with the stuff. Although she enjoyed playing with other children (they weren't usually thrilled, but she had fun), Amber didn't have the attention span to keep busy or play on her own. Barbies might hold her attention for a few fleeting moments, but then she'd be off and running, looking for somebody else's business to get into.

Of course, as she grew, Amber's ability to concentrate increased somewhat. There were a few things she could focus on for a spell (certain cartoons, video games, and her much-prized Cabbage Patch Kids collection), but still her attention span was remarkably short. We always had to allow for the drifting from task to task and thought to thought. We picked up on activities that Amber liked, remembering all the while to present school work, music lessons, and games in small doses. Like most primary and intermediate students of the time, Amber loved stickers, and she had a vast array in her collection. Since it permitted a lot of extraneous interaction, sticker collecting was a good activity for Amber: it allowed her to sort stickers, put them in a book, phone other youngsters about them, run about from place to place to trade them, and so on. Sticker collecting was tailor-made for her hyperactive style.

From the start, Amber loved playing with other children. However, her feelings in this regard weren't always reciprocated—it was hard on the others. Because of her volatile, unpredictable behavior, playmates found it a trying experience to interact with Amber. Few could keep up, and most were only too glad to make their escape as soon as possible. Thus, we were soon into the bouncing from "friend" to "friend" routine.

We found, through the years, that Amber would occasionally focus on some very odd things. One activity that held her attention, especially during confined times (driving in a car, at a movie theater, or in a restaurant) was counting items, such as telephone poles, ceiling lights, or the white whiskers in her Dad's beard. (There were 78 at first count, when Amber was 10 years of age, but the number has grown substantially since then, chiefly because of her.) Once she reached early adolescence, this counting phenomenon manifested itself in a different way. Amber was quite excited about "deforming" (she meant "developing" physically), and—with her motor mouth—she would share every development with us. Amber has never been particularly inhibited, but the running pubic hair count took us aback.

As Amber approached her teens, we were somewhat concerned that she had never really learned to play on her own. Although she maintained some interest in her Cabbage Patch Kids, they didn't hold her for long. Still, they at least gave her something to carry around, dress and undress repeatedly, tug back and forth, and talk to the other kids about. It wasn't quite natural, but it was play of sorts. Keeping the Piagetian stages in mind, we were worried Amber might miss a vital step in her development. Social play is one thing, but a child should eventually be able to play independently. Actually, it wasn't until she was 12 that Amber settled down enough to play with the Barbie Dolls. (In despair, we had sold them all at garage sales years before, so we had to scurry about frantically buying them back.) Feeling that it wouldn't hurt her to go through this stage, we encouraged the Barbie thing again. Her interest didn't last long, only a few months, but this time around Amber was able to play by herself in a more meaningful way. In our view, it was a necessary part of her development, and we're glad she got the chance to play with her dolls, albeit a few years late.

Amber has always been, and remains, immature in many respects. Now, at 25, she can sometimes be extraordinarily insightful and wise, showing a very sophisticated outlook. On many other occasions, though, she exhibits highly immature behavior—so much so that it's a central feature of her personality. Importantly, Amber recognizes the immaturity, acknowledges it, and doesn't worry about it. In a way, her naiveté is refreshing and endearing. Sometimes we wonder if "maturity" isn't an overrated trait. In Amber's case, we're sure her childlike approach will keep her young forever.

Even in her mid-teens, Amber would sometimes carry stuffed toys—which she liked because they were so "cuddable"—to the movies. And she didn't worry about what people thought. While it seemed odd in certain respects, it also showed a strange strength of character. In some ways, Amber is susceptible to influence, but in others she is strangely resistant to peer pressure. Amber is still insufferably pleased with her Cabbage Patch collection, and any room she frequents soon ends up being decorated in a magnificent Mickey Mouse motif. Since Amber shares her Mickey Mouse fetish with her father, one can hardly be critical of her on that account. When all is said and done, we believe that Amber's odd interests, collectables, and gregarious, "social butterfly" nature all help her to cope with her hyperactive world—she needs a lot of little things to keep her amused.

Distractibility

One fact about Amber has remained remarkably constant over the years: with her short attention span, she has great difficulty finishing tasks both at home and at school. As indicated, she drifts from interest to interest quickly, and, in conversation, from topic to topic. Even at mealtime, Amber needs diversions. It invariably takes her far longer to eat a meal than anyone else, largely because any little thing—from interesting tidbits of conversation to a telephone ring, a knock on the door, a noise on television, or the arrival of her pets—sets her off. Typically, when other family members have just about finished up their meals, Amber, though she has been at the table the entire time, is barely starting.

In school, one can imagine how annoying and pervasive this distractibility can be. It's not that Amber doesn't learn, for, in a social sense, she seems to know what is going on in class. She minds everybody's business but her own, she somehow manages to get a feeling for what is happening in every corner of the room, and she acquires some general knowledge, as if by osmosis. Unfortunately, the things she learns usually have nothing to do with what is being taught, or with what she is supposed to learn.

Such distractibility can cause other problems as well. To illustrate, imagine our anxiety when Amber, at 16, decided she wanted to learn to drive. We had always been careful never to mention the words *driver's license* in her presence; we didn't want to face the issue or get her interested. The kid can't even walk from point A to point B without getting sidetracked. How could she pay attention long enough to drive further than a block or two? Luckily for the motorists and pedestrians of Manitoba, Amber eventually realized that she wasn't ready for driving. Rather than become a menace to self and others, she decided, wisely, to hold off until she turned 20. Even then, we didn't feel that Amber was ready for the road, or vice versa. After she passed her formal test, however, she was content to build her skills slowly by always driving with her parents, her brother, or her partner Corey, all of whom supervise very carefully. Now, Amber is up to making a few independent, but relatively short trips each month. We still worry (she really is too easily distracted), but we're becoming more comfortable. The gradual, patient approach has paid dividends.

Impulsivity

We can vouch for the fact that Amber acts before thinking: she is literally hell-on-wheels on a bicycle, she has a go-go-go attitude, and she consistently makes impetuous decisions. Even if we can keep her settled for a spell, she usually picks the most inopportune time to start up again. Once, when Amber was three years old, she managed to annoy the apartment residents by dashing out, without Mom's knowledge, and bringing home the Saturday newspapers (which were left in front of every door) of all the other occupants. To add a little spice to her sojourn, she set out naked on this paper-raiding expedition. Obviously, the neighbors were seriously displeased. This episode was particularly upsetting for Mom, who always watched Amber closely. However, on this particular occasion, Mom was laid low by a headache, and Amber escaped. Relaxing one's vigilance for even a minute could have dire consequences where Amber was concerned.

When Amber started school, she continued to behave rashly, without any thought to consequences. One day after kindergarten, she went off with an adult stranger to visit 7-Eleven. As it turned out, there was no harm intended, but everyone was extremely worried and angry.

During her early school years, Amber also showed a penchant for artwork—she'd impulsively crayon anywhere. When we first brought Amber to the hospital for assessment, the psychiatrist wanted to meet privately with us as parents. We suggested it might not be a good idea to leave our daughter alone for any length of time. But, in his infinite wisdom, the doctor felt that we could confine her safely in a small room, with paper and crayons, for a few minutes. With a sense of foreboding, we complied. After all, we had warned him. Returning from our interview 15 minutes later, we found quite a spectacle. There was no high furniture or climbing apparatus in the sparse office in question, or we might well have had a Sistine Chapel situation. As it was, Amber availed herself of the unexpected opportunity and took the liberty of coloring—in a manner that would have done Michelangelo proud—an impressive mural all over the walls and floor. The psychiatrist was displeased, but the point was made—Amber was tough to manage.

Back at the home front in the apartment, Amber also produced one of her famous murals. However, Mom got the better of her that time, by asking (in a very pleasant tone) which dear child had done the beautiful drawing. Amber admitted to it proudly and, having been so grossly deceived, received swift comeuppance.

A few years later, Amber felt the need to determine whether or not Dad had "ripped off" Mom during their courting years. You can imagine how gratified Mom was to find that her diamond engagement ring was indeed real. Amber had put the question to the test by checking to see if the stone would scratch glass. It did—long, deep scratches. Although Dad's credibility remained intact after the experiment, our once lovely bathroom mirror would never be the same!

Considering the frequency of her ill-thought-out actions, can you imagine our trepidation when we got Amber her first two-wheeler? We spent many days preparing her, drilling in the rules of the road and taking many upon many trial runs around the neighborhood. Still, knowing Amber's tendencies, we were always a little worried. Even though she had the best of intentions, every now and again Amber would, despite the ingrained safety rules, swerve dangerously on her bike or pull out from between parked cars. Amber is quite agile, which allows her to extricate

herself from many predicaments. Still, as the literature suggests, things have caught up with her: she has had her share of accidents, including bike spills, gashes, stitches, severe shoulder and knee injuries, and a dangerous roof shingle to the eye.

What is especially galling is Amber's ability to get us, as well as herself, into trouble. We recall vividly one incident in her grade 6 year, when Amber, despite multiple warnings, wandered off from our house toward the flatlands by the river. Being alert for this sort of thing (we heard Amber's voice from below), Dad—in a very impatient frame of mind—grabbed Chris's bike and rode hell-bent-for-leather toward the riverbank. His agitation was profound, and it was soon to increase. Chris, in an effort to emulate Olympic cyclists, had disengaged the brakes. As Dad slammed them on at the top of the hill, nothing happened. The bike went careening, with him aboard, down the slope. After being battered about unbelievably, and almost plunging into the drink, Dad was fit to be tied (particularly after he found Amber continuing on her merry way, quite unconcerned that her father had almost had the biscuit). Naturally, the two had a calm, heart-to-heart discussion about the incident.

Even when Amber isn't in full flight herself, her actions still cause us grief in an indirect way. In her first year of junior high, there was a little scheduling mix-up; Dad had to hit the road for a business appointment before Mom, who had been delayed, could get back to town. Chris was away playing basketball, so we were faced with the frightful necessity of leaving Amber on her own. Since we had communicated by phone, we knew that there was only going to be about a five-minute shortfall, but leaving Amber by herself even for so short a time filled us with dread. Dad, who simply had to make the appointment, had an intense briefing session with her. She was told not to get into anything, not to cook, and basically not to move for a few minutes until Mom arrived. Having assured himself that everything was copacetic, Dad hurried to the garage, hopped in the van, and began to back out. All of a sudden, he heard screams of "Daddy, Daddy, Daddy!" With nerves taut, and with the vision of a terrible accident already having befallen, Dad reacted abruptly, only to back the vehicle—with a sickening crunch—into the side of the garage. He looked up in desperation to see Amber, standing in the doorway, blowing him a kiss good-bye. Just another day at the McCluskey's.

Excitability

Part of Amber's aforementioned immaturity includes poor emotional control. With her almost childlike outlook and volatility, Amber has always been excitable—to the nth degree. This excitability kept her in ongoing trouble, as she forever argued with other kids over trivial matters (which seemed terribly important to her).

Amber gullibly believes whatever she is told. She is easy to set up and manipulate, and therefore, has usually been blamed for most problems at home and at school. In fairness to her teachers and ourselves as parents, Amber was usually responsible—but not always. Still, because she was so easily victimized by more sophisticated peers, she almost always took the rap. Certainly, her brother at home and other students at school found it simple to shift the blame in her direction. As with other ADHDers, scapegoating was a major problem.

In elementary school, whenever Amber got into a conflict or harangue with another student, she would become extremely emotional, going "wingy" in a desperate attempt to explain her side of the story. She'd often become so excited that she'd say things that simply didn't make sense. Her view and accounts of situations, while containing some elements of truth, would get so distorted as to seem totally implausible. Usually her overall presentation would be so scattered, inconsistent, and preposterous that no one put much stock in anything she had to say.

Amber's excitability and preoccupation with her own viewpoint has sometimes caused serious problems. One example involves Chris's allergic reaction to walnuts. For us, the situation is frightening. Chris's allergy is life threatening—if he eats a walnut, it could well kill him. In fact, Chris begins to react and puff up if a walnut is brought into close proximity. One day, when both kids were in primary school, we took them shopping for groceries at our local supermarket. Chris, always a big boy for his age, had been tormenting Amber throughout the day. In a real flap and armed with her walnut knowledge, she decided to retaliate in the store. We turned around to find one large youngster fleeing wildly for his life, with his little demon sister close behind waving a walnut. In a moment of excitability, Amber had tried to strike back, and she meant business.

When it came to "dating" in late junior and early senior high, Amber was notorious for wearing her heart on her sleeve. With her unrestrained, emotional outlook, she is "affect incarnate". Amber does try to control her emotions, but mostly they get the better of her. One downside here is her mean streak. Most of us manage to rein in our nasty thoughts to some extent, but—with Amber—when she's mad, she's mad (and prone to lash out in a vindictive way at times). Invariably, Amber regrets such episodes and tries to make amends, but she continues to flare up, in unladylike fashion, periodically.

It really is something to see Amber vent her excitable wrath upon unsuspecting victims. Usually we have to urge her to tone it down and keep a civil tongue in her head, but she has a refreshing honesty about her that is sometimes useful. In one memorable situation, we were glad to turn her loose. In December, 1993, Amber and Mom were in a car that was literally stalked and hit by a drunk driver. They were lucky to get out alive. When confronted by the unrepentant culprits in the other vehicle, Amber fired away, letting them know in no uncertain terms that she disapproved of their drinking and driving habits, and of their very existence (and that's a polite euphemism for what she really said). In that case, and in some others, we feel Amber expressed herself well and said things that needed saying. All too often, though, she comes out with comments that would be better left unspoken.

On a positive note, Amber can be oh so much fun in her happy moods, for she gets all excited and appreciative over little details that most of us miss. It's one of the delightful aspects of her personality. Her *joie de vivre* and overall enthusiastic outlook is, despite all the problems, a wonderful thing to behold. However, when threatened, confused, or agitated, Amber has trouble containing herself. With age, she's trying hard to settle down and maintain control, but the excitability is ever present and lurking close to the surface. In many situations, Amber is still simply emotion on legs.

Disorganization

Like so many parents of ADHD children, we've spent our share of time at the lost-and-found. As a young school child, Amber was so disorganized that it was impossible to keep her on track no matter how hard we tried. Her room at home was messy; not regular messy, but hyperactive messy. She would toss things to and fro, arrange and rearrange everything a million times, and generally wreak havoc. Even her most treasured possessions, some of which she truly cherished, could be found outside in the rain, down by the riverbank, at relatives' homes, and generally scattered throughout the country.

A warning signal concerning Amber's disorganization surfaced in her preschool years. Amber had a couple of pet fish, her pride and joy, which she felt (in childhood innocence) were looking a trifle warm. To cool them down for just a second, she put them in the fridge. However, in her inimitable fashion, Amber forgot about them. It was "By an accident, Mom," but decidedly hard on the fish.

Amber's disorganized, scattered behavior was also hard on her father, who was left traumatized by one of her whimsical actions. For a few mornings running, he had noticed that his toothbrush seemed wet even before he had used it. At first, Dad didn't think much about the situation, assuming he had run water over it and forgotten. However, after a few days of this, he knew something was amiss (and assumed Amber was using the wrong brush, an annoying but minor offense). Imagine the disgust when Dad descended the stairs a few days later, to see Amber, with his toothbrush, brushing her dog's teeth! To this day, he refuses to leave his brush in the communal holder in the washroom; it's stored in the top drawer of the dresser for safekeeping.

Amber's disorganization had all kinds of implications in the school setting. Her organizational problems have been, at times, highly debilitating, for she never has what she's supposed to have on hand. Even in her final year of high school, Amber couldn't keep her things straight: she was forever losing her books, her reports, her assignments, or whatever. In her earlier years, watching out for such lapses became almost a full-time job for us. Amber misplaced clothes (one would think it impossible to lose one's pants during the course of a day, but she managed it), toys, homework, and food. At her junior high, we were once accused by school personnel of being neglectful—they believed we weren't providing our daughter with lunch. In all honesty, however, there was a real difference between Amber having a lunch when she left home and having it at noon. One day we were positive that we had sent Amber to school with a slice of cold pizza, but, since she had somehow mislaid it, she had to go, yet again, without lunch. The infamous pizza didn't turn up for a couple of weeks, but we eventually proved it did exist by finding it compressed between the pages of her binder (which shows how often she looked at her school work). To put it succinctly, disorganization has become a way of life in our home; the most we can hope for now is to put a little bit of organization into the overall disorganized scheme of things.

Even today, Amber's home is often a disaster area. However, there has been some improvement. She now has periods of frenzied cleaning to go with her periods of messiness. Still, the fact that she has to change ten times a day, and fling her clothes all over, doesn't help the situation.

In senior high, we struggled to keep Amber on track by using date books, planners/organizers, homework sheets, and study schedules. As she has grown older and somewhat more mature, these have had some effect, but the impact overall has still been rather limited. Sometimes her disorganized and confused style is part of rather a charming demeanor. We were dumbfounded, and pleased, when Amber suddenly asked us during her grade 10 year, "How will I know when I'm sexually active?" That question almost symbolizes her confused, ingenuous approach.

Peer Relationship Problems

In common with many other ADHDers, Amber has a tough time with peer relations. As a young girl, she desperately wanted friends, but she behaved so inappropriately that she couldn't hold on to them. Because she couldn't play well alone, Amber quickly turned into a social butterfly—a very active one, since some of her unwilling targets fled the moment she came into view. At times, her social nature can be appealing (especially now that she is older), but Amber has been hard on many would-be friends.

In her preschool years, Amber loved playing with other children. Although she would often be rebuffed, Amber didn't truly understand what was going on: she just kept plodding ahead in a vain, but contentedly energetic attempt to make new friends. When she reached school age, however, Amber began to realize that she didn't quite fit and that the other kids didn't like her. Because she needed friends so badly, Amber gravitated toward anyone who would have her (and the only ones who would were, from a parental perspective, highly "undesirable"). The youngsters who gave her the time of day typically had serious problems of their own. It was awfully hard for us to find what we would consider acceptable friends for Amber, because she usually turned acceptable people off.

Further, and disconcertingly for us, Amber exhibited another behavior typical of ADHD—she lied a great deal. Although we strove mightily to work on this problem, our daughter—throughout her elementary and junior high years in particular—was apt to blurt out the first thing that came to her mind, and it was very likely to be a patently absurd lie. By continually telling ridiculous falsehoods, Amber quickly ran afoul of both peers and adults.

Certainly, we had ample evidence—teacher comments, parental phone calls of complaint, and direct statements from other children—that Amber wasn't popular with students or staff. At school, she was given the unkind nickname "Godzilla". One day, Amber announced proudly that a boy in her grade 1 class "liked" her. Skeptical (as always where Amber was concerned), we asked how she had come to this conclusion. Amber, in her self-satisfied fashion, replied confidently that she knew she was liked because he called her a "dipstick". Ah, young love!

One characteristic that was especially anxiety arousing for us was Amber's gullibility. In an effort to relate to others, she accepted anything kids told her, as long as they would be her friends. It became disturbing: Amber would believe stories from other youngsters, no matter how ludicrous, and ignore her wonderfully wise parents. Although not harmful, an example arose in grade 2, when Amber, suddenly becoming aware of physiological matters, asked what certain parts of the female body were called. Answering openly and honestly, as good parents should, we replied, "breasts" (and a lecture to prepare her for future developments). A few days later, Amber came raging into the house like a hurricane, quite upset with us for providing misinformation. When we tried to defend ourselves, she confronted us loudly, shouting in no uncertain terms that, "They're not breasts. They're tits 'cause Tanya told me!" Obviously, she had found a more reliable source.

In any case, we had to watch that Amber didn't try to buy friends by bribing them with candies or money. Much of her school life was spent ricocheting from one potential companion to another. Even when Amber was on the periphery of peer group activities, however, she still benefited from her unenduring relationships. Short friendships were better than none at all, for they at least gave her an opportunity to practice and develop her thin repertoire of social skills.

With time, we're pleased to say that Amber has done better in this regard, but the situation remains far from perfect. We've tried to teach her to think more about what she says and does, and a consistent approach over the years has reduced the lying and stealing. Happily, many of the more serious transgressions have essentially disappeared. Still, there's no denying that Amber continues to run into the odd social problem due to her short attention span, distractibility, excitability, and lack of self-control.

In her late junior and senior high school years, Amber found a vehicle for friendship-making through sports. In the early grades, she had all kinds of trouble with complex games (usually coming home in despair after athletic contests because of some incident or another). With baseball, for example, Amber was one of those who could never wait for a full count; she'd be in there swinging before the ball was even pitched. Due to her impulsivity and inability to follow rules, Amber didn't begin playing organized sports until well into grade 9, when she took up basketball. Her instant stardom came at the right time, but she definitely couldn't have handled all those rules earlier. Basketball and football (she was the only female to play on a boys' midget football squad in Manitoba in 1992) gained Amber plenty of attention and helped her to find some good friends. There have been difficult incidents, largely of her own making, and enemies along the way as well. However, we don't mind a few enemies—we're used to that. As long as there are some friends tossed in as a balance, it represents substantial progress.

A particularly unnerving period for us came in secondary school, when Amber started to "date". If we hadn't realized before that she was socially accident-prone, it was driven home then. In his capacity as Director of Special Services for the school district at the time, Dad was aware of most problem-students—all referrals crossed his desk. And the names of referred students were entered on computer and in *The Blue Book*. One fine day, Amber came waltzing home from school and announced joyfully that she had "a new boyfriend". We asked his name, and then cringed. My God, he was an out-and-out sociopath listed in *The Blue Book!* We discouraged this connection, but soon after Amber was back again, deliriously happy about another new beau. "What's his name, Amber?" we asked, waiting for the axe to fall. It did; she had latched on to a confirmed delinquent. The next prospective suitor was a young man who had cut off a cat's ears and drowned the animal in the toilet. Great! We couldn't let a lonely girl go out on dates (she has nice ears), and we couldn't reveal the true reason for her "confinement". It wasn't until grade 11 that things began to look up. Finally, the name of one of the boys Amber was interested in wasn't in the dreaded *Book!* Perhaps she was becoming more discerning. Our relief was short-lived, however, as the individual in question was referred the following Tuesday!

Sometimes, Amber's talkative nature can be a plus. Because she has "been there", she has great sympathy for the down-and-outers. In fact, she has become the self-appointed defender of special needs students, and she will be staunch—and articulately vocal—in that defense, no matter what the cost. When certain "clowns" insist on making life miserable for others less fortunate than themselves, Amber jumps in with alacrity. Her compassion for people with special needs is genuine and winning, and she sticks vehemently to her guns. If she is made mock of or turned upon herself, so be it—she'll hold firm and stay true to her convictions.

Similarly, Amber will take the time to listen sincerely to the problems of others, and offer her own brand of counseling in a forthright, directive way. Frequently, her advice is appreciated; the alternatives she comes up with can be original, creative, and insightful. It's still not uncommon, though, for Amber to make mistakes by responding before thinking. To use her own phrase, she too often reacts spontaneously and "plays it by mouth", rather than planning systematically.

During one incident, we had reason to be pleased with Amber's annoying behavior. In the midst of a basketball game in a foreign gym, she became justifiably incensed because of racial slurs being cast in the direction of one of her teammates. In her role of defending the underdog, Amber—loaded for bear—began to stomp around the court, even though the "victim" was cool and well able to take care of herself. Still, it's one of those things that happen that shouldn't happen, and we were glad to see Amber offended. However, her aggressive style became so marked that she, in turn, became a target for barbs from some of the uncouth fans. It's not always wise to consign your opponents and their supporters to a place of great heat. As Amber was approaching the line to take a foul shot, several of the more obnoxious patrons began to get on her, screaming, "She's no good; she's from out of town! She can't shoot! Air ball, air ball! Small town hicks can't play!" Amber, amid the clamor, advanced calmly to the line, swished the shot through, and, in the brief space of silence that ensued, made her voice heard throughout the gym as she announced smugly, "I'm originally from Winnipeg." She was ready to take on everybody in the place.

With her uninhibited mien, Amber doesn't have many secrets and, as she readily admits, she isn't easily embarrassed. Therefore, with her permission, we'll relate some of the juicier items. Oddly (at least we find it odd), Amber tells us everything about everything. Perhaps due to her motor mouthitis, she just can't help herself. Amber gave us advance warning when she felt she was ready for sex and, since she wanted the first time to be special, we were informed that she had picked Canada Day (no boy, but the day) for the great event. That wasn't hard to handle—we simply locked her up for several Canada Days in succession.

However, during a very sincere attempt at a relationship in her late teens, Amber did finally have her first "close encounter" with a member of the opposite sex. Of course, that very night, she told us all about it, noting that she was nervous, but "not all that uncomfortable"—we literally were given a blow-by-blow account. Some days later, the young man in question slept over, alone in the guest bedroom you can be sure. However, the following morning, a Sunday as it happened, there was a revealing verbal interchange. Often, to get a bit of parental breathing space, the two of us go out alone for Sunday breakfast (once the kids reached late adolescence, we felt we had earned that respite). For whatever reason, that particular Sunday we decided to stay home and have toast and coffee downstairs at the kitchen table. However, upstairs, Chris, Amber, and her consort all assumed we had followed our usual pattern and left for breakfast. Amber, rising first, wandered in to wake her guest, and, sublimely unconscious of the fact it isn't precisely normal behavior, shared with him that she had discussed their escapade with us in depth. Despite our concern over the whole matter, we couldn't help but smile (actually we convulsed with laughter) when we heard his high, falsetto scream from above: "You told them what? Can't you ever keep your mouth shut!" We've always known the answer. It's a resounding "No!"

Learning Problems

It is not surprising that Amber, in common with most ADHD children, had serious learning problems in school. Her behavior—the daydreaming, the verbal and motoric tangents, and the constant buzzing around the classroom—interfered markedly with learning. When we moved from the city for Amber's grade 2 year, we did so partly to help her escape from her "rep"—she had been far and away the most disruptive student in kindergarten and grade 1. After the first few days of grade 2, however, she stated proudly that there was another student in the class, a young boy, who was even "badder than me". Although perhaps ignoble, as parents we were devoutly thankful for the existence of that little guy. Suddenly, Amber wasn't Public Enemy Number One.

In Amber's case, there were in fact some signs of learning problems or disability, particularly reversals. She took a long time to grasp the *b*/*d* and *p*/*q* distinctions, she would reverse numbers such as 3, 4, 6, and 9, and she frequently made ordering errors (producing 61 for 16, and so on). However, Amber's problems were, in effect, quite "soft", for—if she could stay alert—she would frequently spot her mistakes and self-correct. Although she exhibited fairly pronounced reversals (in reading and printing) up to grade 6 and beyond, these have now resolved for the most part. Every now and again, there's some backsliding; Amber still has to concentrate not to reverse, invert, or otherwise confuse material.

Many educators have by now heard their share of cruel jokes concerning learning disabled individuals (who read "Is there a dog?", "Dyslexics of the world untie", etc.). With Amber, we've seen plenty of examples of similar miscues, including ordering mixups, directionality problems, and reversals. In the view of the first author, children inherit their problems from their mothers, and our most striking examples of left-right confusion come not from Amber, but from her Mom. A notable incident took place at Anaheim Stadium in 1992, while the two of us were watching some cheerleaders run out on to the field during half-time at a L.A. Rams' game. The young ladies each carried a large cardboard letter, and naturally—since their entrance was made from our left to right—they had to run out in reverse order. At that moment, Dad immediately saw where Amber's problems came from, as her Mom, in the midst of the puzzled assemblage, loudly asked: "SMAR ALs! What team is that?"

As we've said, Amber's reading problems were so pervasive in the early grades that we were told she was likely to be functionally illiterate. Fortunately, she made significant gains over the years, but reading didn't come easy (and, of course, the deficits here affected performance in other school subjects). Even now, after all the progress, Amber mixes passages occasionally and misreads basic material.

Verbally, too, while Amber can be highly articulate, every now and again ordering problems and confusions also slip into her thoughts and her speech. For example, she once referred to Don Quixote's squire, Sancho Panza, as his "kickside" (she meant sidekick). She also desperately needed to have a pair of "knockers" (she meant knickers). Later in her career, we

heard her butchered version of the famous quotation from *Gone with the Wind*, "Frankly, madam, I don't give a deer!" We were equally chagrined when her interpretation of "Jumpin' Jehoshaphat" turned out to be "Jumping Jesus, Joseph's fat". Sir Walter Scott wasn't spared: "Oh what a tangled web we weave, when first we practice to conceive." And Chris was astounded to find that he once scared his sister "out of her foreskin". More recently, she confided to us that her life "flashed before her eyes" during the car accident mentioned earlier. Much to our delight, Amber, in unrestrained exultation, then smirked and stated that she now knew what she was getting for Christmas. We had to explain that it's usually your past, not future events, that flash by on such occasions.

Her problems notwithstanding, even when she was young, we were both convinced that Amber had more than her share of seat-of-the-pants smarts. To us, her abilities seemed to be odd and twisted, but they were there. Sadly, in school, very few people noticed—they were too hung up on the reading and academic problems, and with the disruptive and annoying behaviors.

To reassure ourselves, we ran Amber through a battery of tests during her grade 1 year (when we were getting the dire prophecies about her future). It's the curse of children of psychologists that they end up being tested to death; Amber certainly was. But, as a six-year-old, she demonstrated her potential (though we've never found it easy to tap). On the WISC-R (Wechsler Intelligence Scale for Children – Revised) administered at the time, Amber was asked to indicate how "pound" and "yard" were similar. She didn't realize they were measurements, but hesitated only a moment before responding, "You keep dogs in them." Not technically correct perhaps, but logical. And when looking for missing elements in pictures, Amber was incredibly observant for her age in terms of noticing fine detail. Her keen eye was particularly evident in an item where she was shown a picture of a thermometer, with the mercury missing from the bottom of the bulb. Amber couldn't verbalize the flaw, but she put things her own way by noting, "There's no blood at the bottom!"

When looking at her reading skills, or lack thereof, we once tried to get a measure of Word Attack on the Woodcock Reading Mastery Tests. To start off this particular segment (which involves the presentation of nonsense words such as "wubfambif" and "bafmotbem" for the youngster to decode), one presents the meaningless syllable "tat." We explained to Amber that it wasn't a word, and that she would be faced with other nonsense syllables of this type. Immediately, Amber balked and stated in her recalcitrant tone, "No, that's a word." We replied, "No, Amber, it doesn't mean anything." But she insisted, "No, it's a word!" So we finally asked, "Okay, if it's a word, can you use it in a sentence for us?" She replied smugly, "I tot I taw a puddy tat!"

Over the years, we often got the wisdom-from-the-mouths-of-babes routine from Amber. In grade 3, she noticed, since we tend to live well beyond our means, that we were often in desperate financial straits and presenting something of a false front to the world. At that point, she asked innocently, "Mom and Dad, will we ever have as much money as people think we have?"

Even earlier, when she was eight years of age, we were stunned when Amber, riding along in the car to her music lesson, announced determinedly: "When I grow up, I'm not going to be a prostitute. I plan to have enough money of my own." You can't imagine what this revelation meant to us. In the same vein, on a beautiful, misty, early winter day, Amber, during another car ride, marveled at the beauty of the "prostitute frost". It took us a while to click on, but finally we realized she was referring to the "hoarfrost".

Although we recognized Amber's strengths and unique way of looking at the world, not everyone did. If truth be told, we could easily understand how her teachers might be discouraged; we were discouraged ourselves. At home, realizing that Amber couldn't possibly handle all her academic work, we decided to emphasize reading in the early years. Attempting to do more would have been overwhelming. However, by making this decision, we more or less cast her adrift in terms of writing, spelling, and math. These subjects were left largely to the teachers, even though we knew Amber would be unable to concentrate for more than a fraction of each school day. Our hope, and it has been partly realized, was that with increasing age, maturity, and concentration span she would close the gap later in her academic career.

Even with extra input, Amber, a nonreader through most of grade 3, wasn't a bookworm by any means. Still, by grade 4, she had made a beginning: the constant encouragement, work, and special materials had an effect. By grade 5, Amber was less than two years below grade level in reading. Not bad, considering her very late start.

However, where real concentration was required (e.g., with writing, spelling, and math), the situation remained rather abysmal. In that grade 5 year, it was highlighted to us that Amber's basic skills were far from what they should have been. One day, before heading off for school, she took the time to leave a note for her older brother, who was sick that particular morning. Amber's goal had been to compose a kind, compassionate note, for she can be very considerate at times. She had attempted to print, "Get well soon Chris. From Sweetie Pie." Now where she got off calling herself "Sweetie Pie" we don't know, but that was her intent. Unfortunately, Amber misspelled *sweetie*, and she also misspelled *pie* (as *piy*). Further, exhibiting her usual poor penmanship, she messed up the *y*. The net result was that we picked up a note from the kitchen table that read, "Get well soon Chris. From Sweaty Pig." While such an effort might be humorous at home, we can appreciate that receiving work of this caliber could be distressing for teachers. It was embarrassing for us as parents—Amber was again ripping our reputation to shreds in the educational community.

Teachers could probably have lived with the situation had not Amber's academic weaknesses been accompanied by her overactive behavior. Many tried hard but, through no fault of their own, they had a tough time controlling and teaching Amber. Toward the end of grade 6, we had to make a decision about Amber's future. Heeding the advice of school personnel, we opted for retention. Although we agonized over this choice, looking back, we're pleased we did what we did. Aside from the academic weaknesses, Amber wasn't ready in a social sense. Given her immaturity, she may well have been "eaten alive" had she gone on to junior high that year. Besides, Amber didn't feel awkward at all about being held back; she realized she wasn't prepared for the step up. To this day, we have reason to be thankful for this particular strength in Amber—she'll admit when she's not ready and take her time.

The following year, Amber did move on, but (as in elementary) it didn't take long for us to realize that it would be a struggle to get her through the secondary grades. In fact, in mid-junior high, we recognized the importance of lecturing her on this issue. Realizing that she wouldn't have the luxury of doing the things that some students can get away with (skipping a few classes, forgetting assignments, and the like), we urged Amber to "use every edge" by attending regularly, focusing at all times, and handing in every assignment, no matter how trivial. Naturally, Amber never managed to do any of these things consistently, but we felt the closer she could come to this ideal, the better chance she would have. As a consequence, we really belabored the use-every-edge theme, extending it to include being polite to teachers, staying neat, and otherwise showing good impression management skills. However, shortly thereafter, Amber took us quite literally (as she often does) by walking up to the vice principal and warning, "My Dad is Director of Special Services; it would be best for you if I pass." As always, our advice to Amber ended up causing us embarrassment. We never brought up the edge business again.

In high school, our problems continued, but, happily for our sanity, progress was evident. As Amber put it at the time, "Only some teachers hate me now." Without condoning the behavior of the "haters", we understood—it can be difficult liking her on certain occasions, especially when she gets in one of her moods. However, Amber is trying hard to settle down and, while she still presents a problem for some structured, rigid individuals, others find her quite likable and intriguing. We've had positive comments from several people of late indicating that they recognize the uniqueness, talent, and kindness in Amber. It's not so hard to take the negative when a few positives emerge as well. Also, we were heartened by comments from one of her elementary teachers, who came up to Amber in a restaurant and congratulated her for finishing high school. Apparently, back in the early days, no one thought she had a chance of getting that far. He observed, "She now behaves in an articulate, pleasant, ladylike fashion." And sometimes she does.

We know it will continue to be a struggle, especially since Amber is now poised do something she swore she would never do—try her hand at university. We're optimistic about her chances, since her interest in reading is developing, her talent for public speaking is widely recognized, and her wit is much appreciated. In short, while the weaknesses have not entirely disappeared, the strengths have become more evident; she has a creative foundation on which to build.

Familial Problems

Although we've never quite reached the divorce-due-to-Amber stage, we can attest to the fact that her behavior has put all sorts of pressure on us. There is always trouble revolving about her. Having an Amber forced us to "get our act together" as parents. She was manipulative enough, in a reactive way, to play both ends against the middle, so it was necessary to take a consistent approach at home, at school, with relatives, and in community groups.

Not surprisingly, we often just didn't know what to do with Amber. We tried to develop plans so we were never at a loss, but that proved impossible. She always managed to come up with stunts so startling that we fell back in disarray. When we got hit with such surprises, we learned to stall for time by sending Amber to her room. This sort of time-out allowed her, and us, a moment to cool off. Once we calmed down, the two of us would take a parenting interlude to develop a plan. That is, banishing Amber to her room gave us breathing space to think of unique options to deal with Amber's unique behavior. Believe us, some innovative parenting was required.

Amber's grade 4 year was particularly trying—she aggravated both us and school personnel beyond belief. Basically, our daughter was going to hell in a handbasket academically, to say nothing of her disruptive behavior. At one school meeting, after hearing a litany of accusations, we asked the principal, "Can't you find anything good about this kid?" The answer was, "Frankly, no." We were angry, but in an abstract way, we understood the frustration. Quite simply, Amber was a difficult, difficult case.

Sadly, for parents of ADHDers, frustration on the part of others often results in blaming. Many think you are the cause of the child's horrific behavior. In our situation, we felt the parenting was pretty damn good— there was just something within this girl that made her different. Nonetheless, when you have a youngster who can't behave in school, with friends, at the homes of relatives, or in public, you end up feeling embarrassed and guilty, as if you were somehow responsible for the entire state of affairs. That's why home-school communication becomes so critical when working with hyperactive youngsters. It's important for the parents to realize what a strain this kid may be putting on teachers and other students. Conversely, school personnel must try to understand that the bad behavior is not necessarily the result of a poor home life. By respecting the other point of view, parents and educators can collaborate more effectively and work together, in consistent fashion, to help the child.

In considering family dynamics, one often forgets about the pressure a hyperactive youngster can put on other siblings. Because Amber was so difficult in so many ways, she sometimes drove Chris to distraction. Even though there is only slightly more than a year between them, he was far more mature as a child, which meant he was forever bothered by her "zaniness". When we supported retention for Amber in grade 6, one of our secondary considerations was that we really didn't want to have Amber in grade 7 when Chris was in grade 8. Although they fought like cats and dogs, Chris, in an effort to live up to his brotherly responsibilities, would try to protect his sister when the occasion demanded (and it often demanded). Naturally, he frequently got into hot water because of her. We thought it wouldn't hurt for him to have that extra year of emotional and physical maturity (so that, when he had to intervene on Amber's behalf, he would be in a senior position—in grade 9 in junior high and grade 12 in high school).

Several times, the things that Amber did had a profound affect on her brother. For a brief spell, Chris was so embarrassed that he denied having a sister. After coming to terms with the situation once and for all, however, he eventually became her staunchest defender. To illustrate, in senior high Amber somehow offended a group of "tough" students, who— mirroring the ways of today's world—decided to "get her". Due to Chris's efforts, however, Amber was difficult to get. He literally had her guarded at school by various members of the community football team, a very large, intimidating group. Chris is quite skilled at avoiding confrontation and, for the most part, Amber's protectors followed his lead by supporting her positively, not confrontationally. Still, it put pressure on Chris to gather recruits, set up surveillance, and monitor Amber's whereabouts throughout the day. Many guys on the team were highly supportive—they knew Amber, they knew she was different, and they knew she needed watching. Since, as mentioned earlier, Amber ended up playing for the team herself, they got to know her idiosyncrasies firsthand. Instead of being seen as the embodiment of evil, Amber was viewed compassionately—the boys understood that she needed help, and they provided it (gently, but firmly).

All too often, Chris was placed in a position where he had to support Amber (physically at times, but more often verbally) in dicey situations. Considering that she had usually caused the situation, it was sometimes hard for Chris to defend her. Nevertheless, despite the embarrassment and frustration, he generally did his best, earning our grateful thanks that there has been a watchdog at hand. And forever trying to extricate Amber has, in the end, provided Chris with a variety of social and interpersonal skills which are now helping immeasurably in his budding teaching and coaching career. Having dealt from an early age with the most difficult binds imaginable, anything in the future should be a piece of cake for him.

ADHD behavior has implications for all family members, including pets. Ours were always being bathed, dressed up, made over, or badgered unceasingly. Amber loves animals dearly and, because she lavishes nonstop, hyperactive affection on them, they love her in return. However, she is sometimes a sore trial even to them. Poor Sprite, one of the cats, really suffered; being female she was made up frequently. In one entertaining episode, Amber (while in junior high) had put the poor feline in a yellow dress and a special bonnet. To complete the effect, she did Sprite's eyes and plastered a ghastly shade of green lipstick all over her mouth. Amber was carrying her dolled-up cat through the back yard, when an unsuspecting dog wandered on to the scene. Sprite, who was highly territorial, leapt into action and attacked furiously. The confused dog, looking up to see this hideous apparition bearing down upon it, fled in abject terror.

The point is that hyperactivity does not occur in isolation; it affects everyone in the immediate vicinity. We saw an example at a "social" several years back. Amber was thrilled because an unaware, uninitiated young man had actually asked her out, and she brought him along to this family event. About midway through the evening, Amber took a little stroll outside with her date. Naturally, since we never take our eyes off her, the two of us noted their departure. After waiting only a few minutes, we started to rise to check on our daughter—we've learned not to give her the time to get herself into trouble. However, before we could bestir ourselves, Chris and his cousins Devron and Duwayne, football players both, sauntered past our table and informed us that Amber had left with "this guy". The boys had just taken a quick look outside, and things were okay. They'd keep checking. A moment later, Gramma and Grampa McCluskey strolled over to alert us that Amber had gone outside—hadn't we better take a walk in that direction? As it turned out, Gramma and Grampa Parisian had already been on a reconnaissance mission of their own; they stopped by our table to let us know that the two young people were "just talking". Then Uncle Darrell, an imposing fellow, came up to tell us that Amber had gone outside and that things were okay, he had gone out to chat with her. And, finally, Uncle Bradley, a formidable figure in his own right, reported that he had talked to the two kids to make sure that there was "no funny business going on out there". Before we received an update from every relative in the place, we decided to bring Amber and her friend back in; undoubtedly, they'd get more privacy in the crowded hall. Amber returned pliably enough, but she had to guide her stunned guest back to their seats—he looked singularly bemused and harassed. We never saw him again.

As she approached adulthood, Amber found this constant watching out for her to be rather vexing; she had an overly large complement of "keepers". It did take some time for us to learn to loosen up a bit. However, we don't feel too bad about her vexation; with all the aggravation she has caused us and others, it's only fair that we got in a few shots of our own. Besides, while this overprotection might have been annoying, it showed Amber that a lot of people do care about her.

Low Self-Concept

It's not unnatural for hyperactive children to have notoriously low self-concepts. Indeed, it only makes sense. After ongoing school failure, unpopularity with teachers and classmates, incident upon incident, and negative messages year after year, there's bound to be some impact on self-image.

That such children usually acquire "bad reps" exacerbates the situation. In Amber's case, she was almost invariably blamed for everything. She was usually guilty, but on the few occasions when she wasn't, she was still raked over the coals. From her point of view as a child, there was no use being good—she was going to get into trouble no matter what.

As we've said, during her early years, Amber's hyperactivity and behavior weren't really a concern to her personally—she didn't understand precisely what was going on. In essence, she was a "pain in the ass" (a clinical term for ADHD) for everyone else, but her behavior wasn't an issue for her.

However, as she grew (and continued to run into problems at home, at school, and with her friends), Amber began to realize how different she was. In grade 3, there was an episode that tore at our heartstrings. We were called to school, yet again, because Amber had been involved in an incident on the playground: she was caught kissing an ugly stray dog. We were thoroughly put out by her behavior, and in our family meeting with the principal asked her, "Why Amber? Why this final ignominy? Why were you kissing the stupid dog?" Her response broke our hearts: "It's my only friend!"

Further self-realization of her problems came in grade 6, when, in frustration one morning, Amber wandered into the kitchen to ask us to please help her concentrate. She wanted to be put on medication to

increase her attention span. Not being particularly sensitive that AM (it was a bad parenting day), and not realizing just how distraught she was, we brushed Amber aside, saying that medication wasn't always the answer. Amber expressed annoyance at her father, asking, "What kind of psychologist are you anyway?" Thinking she was just in one of her moods, we didn't pick up on the full measure of her distress.

Since we had resisted medication, Amber came up with a scheme of her own. That day at school, she went to see her new principal, and, in tears, tried to explain her dilemma and ask for help. Amber stated, in a trembling voice, that she just couldn't concentrate. Specifically, she said: "Mrs. Phillipson, if a fly is buzzing around the room, of course I have to watch it. Then, if it lands on my desk, I still have to watch it. If it moves across my ruler, I need to watch it. And when it flies off, I just can't stop watching it. I can't ever concentrate!" Still sobbing, Amber went on to request that teachers cut out some large pieces of cardboard and set up a makeshift barrier around her desk (to shield her from outside distractions and help her stick to task). Amber intended to ask to be "isolated". In her jumbled style, though, she chose the wrong word and asked instead to be "sterilized". Luckily, Mrs. Phillipson sorted everything out.

While this story is humorous and touching, Amber was clearly disturbed that she was different and not doing well. Nowadays, she is much more inclined to ask for help, but in elementary and junior high, she often felt that her situation was hopeless. Amber, like so many ADHD youngsters, took a tremendous emotional battering. We tried to provide a buffer from the attacks (and attacks they were, though often well-intentioned) by giving plenty of emotional support at home. Many's the time outsiders would get annoyed with us, feeling that we weren't tough enough on our daughter. They were wrong; we were plenty tough when we had to be. However, one can't control each instant, tighten up everything, or force a hyper kid to become a model child. If we hadn't provided a safe base, our girl wouldn't have had a childhood. For self-esteem to remain intact, overactive children need unconditional affection, security, and love—no matter what they may do. And often, if they don't get those essential ingredients at home, they won't get them anywhere. It is critical that parents work on behavior, provide guidelines, and tighten the reins when necessary, but they must never withdraw emotional support from their ADHD children.

*Amber and Chris in early childhood
and early adulthood.*

Chapter 4

COPING WITH HYPERACTIVITY

When thinking about Amber's "condition", two quotations come to mind. The first is the well-known adage: "Grant me the serenity to accept the things I cannot change; courage to change the things I can, and wisdom to know the difference." Although she was often nigh on impossible, we needed to acquire wisdom enough to realize that Amber was Amber. Nothing we were going to do would turn her into a paragon of virtue overnight. Besides, we didn't necessarily want a paragon. We've come to appreciate Amber (a.k.a. Amber-Lee, Am, Berg, Cumquatling, or Baby Girl Tiger) the way she is. However, we did want to find ways to control the blemishes and enlarge the virtues.

The second quote is one we've heard attributed to Twain: "Don't try to teach a pig to sing. It won't work, and besides, you'll annoy the pig." That maxim has something to say to us about accepting our fate and Amber's "way of being". Try as we might, it has always been tough to get Amber to behave as she ought. Going one step further, there were certain things that we might expect from other youngsters that were not fair to expect from Amber. She simply could not comply. Sitting still, for example, was not part of her makeup; she couldn't do it. From the outset, then, we decided to broaden our notions of discipline and soften our goals. Rather than ask Amber to do things that she found impossible, we tried to modify and set realistic expectations. This is not to say that we abandoned discipline or abdicated responsibility; far from it! As much as possible, we endeavored to treat Amber the way we treated other children. However, we kept enough flexibility in our approach to allow for her individual foibles. Flexible discipline—that's the key.

An Interactive, Integrated Approach

Interactive, multidimensional, integrated approaches to treatment recognize the need to plug into hyperactivity on several fronts. Obviously, there are many perspectives to consider in the diagnosis and treatment of attention deficit: personal, parental, educational, and medical. ADHDers, parents, teachers, and doctors must tackle the problem together. Like others before us, we support the idea of using a variety of direct and indirect treatment combinations to address the ADHD issue. By the way, we're not saying that primary symptoms should necessarily be dealt with directly, or secondary symptoms indirectly. It depends. There are no hard and fast rules: it's important to be flexible and to do what makes sense. By working together (and using a variety of approaches for a variety of problems in a variety of settings), the main players can usually ameliorate each individual situation to some extent. However, don't forget that ubiquitous proviso—there are no magic solutions. With ADHD, it's almost always a case of making things better, not perfect. Besides, a perfect world would be extremely bland. And whatever else it may be, life with Amber is never boring.

There are all kinds of mainstream and alternative treatments out there for ADHD (cf. Barkley, 1998; Garshowitz, Hui, Levinson, Lyon, & Marshall, 2001; Goldstein & Goldstein, 1998; Knights & Bakker, 1980; Melmed, 2001; Weyandt, 2001). Some treatments are effective for certain people under certain conditions, others show promise but need more investigation, and others are of dubious worth. Since there are a smorgasbord of possibilities—something for everyone, as they say—it is essential to evaluate carefully and choose wisely from among the options.

No one treatment method solves all the problems. There is usually much more success when a multiple or multimodal approach is put into place: a combination of treatments is likely to have more impact than any one method applied in isolation (Barkley, 1998; DuPaul & Stoner, 1994; Goldstein & Goldstein, 1998; Maté, 1999; Melmed, 2001; Phelan, 1993). By the same token, there must always be a judicious balance. One should not go hog wild, overstimulate, and bombard an ADHD child (Kinsbourne & Caplan, 1979). There is a need to be selective.

Basically, no definitive boundaries exist; symptoms and causes overlap. Therefore, it makes sense that there be overlap and flexibility in treatment. Every case is unique. Each hyperactive person is an individual: it would be a grievous error to treat everybody the same. What works with one child may not work with another, and vice versa. There may well be many treatment shifts (i.e., trying different amounts of different things in different combinations) before an optimal approach is achieved.

Hyperactivity is a long-term problem, so using some highly touted technique for a day or two isn't going to do the trick. In contrast, an incredible amount of time, energy, and painstaking work is required on the part of parents, teachers, and others. And trying to tackle ADHD alone is not the way to go; one almost always needs help. Building on this thought, it's essential that parents have a solid support system available. Significant others (relatives, friends, coaches, etc.) must network to form a cohesive team. If parents of hyper kids are to meet their own needs (and be any good to anyone else), they require some respite. Unless parents of a hyperactive child spell each other off and/or get some assistance from others (so they can spend a bit of time away from their kid), they'll probably burn out. There must be breaks between the bursts of intensive effort.

Over the years, a plethora of books have been produced to help parents understand and cope with ADHD (Alexander-Roberts, 1994, 1995; Amen, 1996; Barkley, 2000; Fowler, 1994; Garber, Garber, & Spizman, 1995; Goldstein & Goldstein, 1986, 1992; Greenberg & Horn, 1991; Hollands, 1983; Ingersoll, 1988; Ingersoll & Goldstein, 1993; Minde, 1988; Moss, 1990; Parker, 1988; Taylor, 1990; Train, 1996; Umansky & Smalley, 1994; Wodrich, 1994). There is even work which considers the role of the father specifically (Jacobs, 1998).

How about from a teacher's perspective? How would you cope with a Robin Williams or a Jim Carey in the classroom? Indeed, a large body of literature is available to help teachers deal with their ADHD students (Connor, 1974; DuPaul & Stoner, 1994; Fairchild, 1975; Friedman & Doyal, 1992; Gadow, 1979; Gadow & Rapport, 1987; Goldstein & Goldstein, 1987; Johnson, 1992; O'Brien & Obrzut, 1986; Oud, 1988; Parker, 1992; Rief, 1993). Some of these and other sources offer information for teachers about monitoring and working with students on medication. Overall, there is a great deal of emphasis placed on using nonverbal and visual cues, specific praise, peer helpers, cooperative approaches, authentic assessment to measure learning, and strategies such as providing choices, simplifying directions, and moving to project-based activities (DuPaul & Stoner, 1994; Parker, 1992; Rief, 1993; Weaver, 1994).

It is especially crucial that parents and educators cooperate with one another (Council for Exceptional Children, 1993; DuPaul & Stoner, 1994; Gordon, 1991; Hemphill, 1996; Learning Disabilities Association of Manitoba, 1999; Moghadam & Fagan, 1994; Parker, 1988; Phelan, 1993).

All too frequently, parents of hyperactive students end up in a negative, adversarial relationship with teachers and school administrators. Actually, it's not surprising that the situation frequently degenerates into unpleasant confrontation. Teachers get frustrated with ADHD children, and naturally blame parents for not providing enough structure and discipline at home. And frustrated parents wonder why teachers aren't more (or less) firm, more caring, and more sensitive to the needs of their child. It's all too easy to blame others, but blaming is counterproductive. Borrowing from the Creative Problem Solving (CPS) literature (Isaksen, Dorval, & Treffinger, 2000; Treffinger, Isaksen, & Dorval, 2000), it makes much more sense to gather information, identify specific problems, and then respond realistically, positively, and meaningfully. By exploring data and looking objectively at the "current reality", parents and teachers can join forces to work through problems together (and reach a more "desired future state").

Over the years, Amber has had many unfortunate experiences at school, but we prefer not to dwell on these. We look at them simply as speed bumps on the road of life—learning experiences, not permanent, scarring setbacks. It is much more uplifting and emotionally profitable to highlight the good things that have happened. From the elementary years, we remember a teacher in grade 3, who, perhaps for the first time, succeeded in making our girl feel part of a class. When Amber was home sick for a few days, Mrs. Dann had all the kids sign and mail a get-well card (they lied and said they missed her.) Amber was ecstatic when that card arrived; it instilled a sense of belonging. From junior high, we remember Mrs. Breznik, who showed mercy and kept mum after catching our daughter cheating (Amber, of course, eventually let the cat out of the bag). Later, Mrs. B. phoned to let us know that Amber would be receiving two basketball awards at the grade 9 "graduation". Teacher and parents were equally thrilled; we knew what this positive public recognition would mean to a girl who had hitherto been singled out only for negatives. And to top things off, Mrs. Breznik presented her old grad gown to Amber for the awards night and dance. Our daughter was deeply moved, and today that same gown hangs in her closet, waiting for the graduation of her daughter Hunter. At the senior high level, we are grateful to many educators who took time, went that extra mile, and occasionally bent the rules a trifle to help Amber make it through. Yes, there were some "downs", but those pale in significance to the "ups" provided by dedicated teachers (who, happily, are too numerous to mention).

Remembering that it takes a system to break a system, parents should also work cooperatively with community caregivers such as Brownie or Cub leaders, coaches, and music teachers. Sometimes, overactive youngsters with a multiplicity of problems are simply thrown into a club or placed on a sports team without any advance warning. If parents take the time to meet with leaders and coaches beforehand (and explain the problems, the child's interests, and techniques that are most effective), people in the community may be able to gear up, plan, and help. They, too, can become part of what should emerge as an informal, multidisciplinary team striving to meet the youngster's needs in a consistent manner.

Once more, we would like to renew our never-ending call for flexibility. There is no right or wrong way; the art of parenting an ADHDer is the ability to shift approaches as circumstances dictate. Most of all, it requires common sense. But as Twain has also said, "Common sense isn't that common." Rather than looking for an all-purpose solution in some mythical text, parents need to assess each situation realistically and make sensible, effective decisions about and with their child. A frantic search for diagnosis and panaceas isn't the answer; a logical, common sense, individualized approach will come closer to the mark.

Don't forget the main players, the ADHDers themselves. Feldhusen (1995) has argued powerfully that students should be involved in and take some responsibility for the development of their own talents. In his view, they must learn to recognize their personal strengths and do something proactive to build upon them. Insofar as attention deficit is concerned, it's also important that children, as they grow, gradually assume more and more ownership for their own behavior. A number of books have been written for children with ADHD to involve them in the treatment process, provide general information (about the disorder, medication, etc.), and offer suggestions for developing study, organizational, listening, friendship, social, and self-control skills (Frank & Smith, 1994; Gehret, 1991; Parker, 1988; Quinn & Stern, 1991; Taylor, 1996).

Children grow up, however, and situations, demands, and ADHD itself change over the course of the lifespan (Hallowell & Ratey, 1994; Moragne, 1996; Phelan, 1993; Wender, 1987; Weiss & Hechtman, 1993). Amber today is not what she was 10 years ago and not what she will be 10 years hence. Recognizing the long-term nature of the disorder, recent "survival" guides have been produced to help adolescents (Children and

Adults with Attention Deficit Disorders, 1996; Hemphill, 1996; Quinn, 1995), college students (Goldstein, 1997; Nadeau, 1994), and adults (Goldstein, 1997; Hallowell & Ratey, 1994; Kelly & Ramundo, 1993; Wender, 1995) cope more effectively with scheduling, organizational and educational issues, and a host of other matters. There is also material dealing with the impact of attention deficit on the family system, marriage, and employment (Fisher & Beckley, 1998). It has been suggested that ADHD adults in the workplace consider seeking alternatives to traditional 9:00–5:00 jobs, and that they concentrate on putting the positive side of hyperactivity to good use (Nadeau, 1997). Similarly, women with ADHD have been encouraged to "embrace" their condition at work and at home (Solden, 1995).

Direct Intervention Strategies

Essentially, when using direct intervention, adults get involved in a very practical and straightforward fashion, doing something, in effect, "to" the child. In other words, with this form of intervention, we're talking about specific treatment. Although the distinction isn't always quite that black and white, for us direct intervention strategies include the following:

Medication

In many cases, the treatment for ADHD is medication, usually stimulants. Again, not being experts in this area, we've relied heavily on the work of others to give us a feeling for the issues (Anastopoulos, DuPaul, & Barkley, 1991; Barkley, 1989, 1998; Carey, 1990; Clements & Peters, 1962; Crenshaw, Kavale, Forness, & Reeve, 1999; Forness, Kavale, & Crenshaw, 1999; Gadow, 1988; Garber, Garber, & Spizman, 1996; Gaynor, 1990; Goldstein & Goldstein, 1998; Greenberg & Horn, 1991; Greenhill & Osman, 1999; Gross & Wilson, 1974; Ingersoll, 1988; Jacobvitz, Sroufe, Stewart, & Leffert, 1990; Johnson, 1988; Kavale, 1982; Maté, 1999; Melmed, 2001; Moghadam, 1988; Oud, 1988; Schwartz & Johnson, 1987; Strauss & Lehtinen, 1947; Swanson, Cantwell, Lerner, McBurnett, & Hanna, 1991; Wender, 1987; Weyandt, 2001).

For well over half a century, Ritalin (methylphenidate) and other stimulants have been used to treat hyperactivity. One might wonder why anybody would give stimulants to an already overactive youngster, but there is a rationale. If there is dysfunction in pathways or transmission in the prefrontal lobe region—the area of the brain which has been termed *the executive function, the impulse control,* or the "whoa down" center—stimulants may activate or restore the inhibitory and attentional mechanisms (so that the ADHDers can, in fact, "whoa down" and gain more focus, awareness, and control over their actions). Because it appears that depletion of neurotransmitters in the frontal lobe may be involved in ADHD etiology, such medication is a logical way to stimulate the "secretary of the brain".

Used most often with children, stimulant medication is now commonly prescribed for adolescents and adults as well. While there are individual differences in reaction to Ritalin, response time is typically 30–45 minutes, with peak effects 2–4 hours after ingestion. Since it's metabolized entirely in 12 hours, there is a rapid decline in the effect. Therefore, to help a child through the school day, Ritalin is usually administered twice, in the morning and at noon. A newer sustained-release form has longer staying power, and, therefore, needs to be given only once a day: its effects, however, are less consistent. Dosage will vary, depending on age, body weight, idiosyncratic response, and other factors.

Alternatives to stimulant medication include the tricyclic anti-depressants, imipramine, desipramine, and nortriptyline. Although these tend to be longer lasting than stimulants, they are much slower acting, frequently less effective, and often the cause of more pronounced side effects. Neurolepic medications are sometimes used, in combination with the tricyclic antidepressants, when major behavioral problems or conduct disorders are involved. And occasionally, antihistamines, anti-epileptic Tegretol, or medications from other groups are employed on a selective basis. Herbal alternatives are also popular in some quarters. But stimulant medication is typically the treatment of choice for attention deficit, with Ritalin being by far and away the most widely prescribed alternative.

A voluminous body of literature points to the positive short-term impact Ritalin has on ADHD children, adolescents, and adults (cf. Barkley, 1998; Crenshaw, Kavale, Forness, & Reeve, 1999; Forness, Kavale, & Crenshaw, 1999; Garber, Garber, & Spizman, 1996; Goldstein, & Goldstein, 1998; Weyandt, 2001). Many studies from the past were poorly controlled and speculative, but there is a wealth of research that has been systematic and objective. Some reviews indicate that Ritalin is helpful in about 75% of the clinical cases examined, and that overactive children show significantly more behavioral improvement with it than with placebos (though placebos can have considerable impact in many instances).

Some of the work has certainly been thorough. Crenshaw, Kavale, Forness, and Reeve (1999), Forness, Kavale, and Crenshaw (1999), and Kavale (1982) have offered the results of meta-analyses done on 135 studies conducted prior to 1980 and on 115 others that took place between 1981 and 1995. Stressing all the while that medication shouldn't necessarily be the first or only treatment for hyperactive children, they nevertheless make the point strongly (through quantitative synthesis of a large volume of data) that stimulant medication is, as a stand-alone intervention, the most effective treatment available. Because it has been demonstrated to have far more impact than psychosocial approaches, these investigators submit that stimulant medication "is probably the key ingredient in successful treatment for ADHD" and should, in fact, "be the primary treatment" (Forness, Kavale, & Crenshaw, 1999, p. 233).

Dexedrine (dextroamphetamine), the main alternative to Ritalin over the years, is another stimulant with similar effects that is available both in fast-acting and sustained-release forms. Cylert (pemoline), yet another stimulant that has been used to treat ADHD children and adolescents, is usually given once daily. However, there have been concerns about its slow acting nature, difficulty in fine-tuning dosage, and side effects (i.e., in rare instances, possible liver damage). In Canada, it is now available only through the emergency drug program.

Since it is a hot market out there, newer stimulant medications, including Concerta and Adderall, have recently appeared on the scene, and more are on the way. Although it's early to draw firm conclusions, Concerta (methylphenidate HCI)—designed to be taken only once a day, in the morning—has been found by some parents and teachers to improve the attention and behavior of ADHDers. Adderall—a combination of amphetamine salts—has been shown, in some studies, to be effective in treating ADHD children and adolescents, including those who reacted negatively or did not respond to Ritalin (Manos, Short, & Findling, 1999; Pliszka, Browne, Olvera, & Wynne, 2000).

Clearly, scores of pediatricians and psychiatrists feel that stimulant medication is a safe, efficient way of improving attention span and decreasing overactivity. Children respond differently, but a large number obviously become more attentive and less hyper when put on meds. Working in the schools as we do, we have seen many, many cases where medication has helped a great deal. With some students we've known, educators had tried everything in their power, with extremely limited success. Medication, as a last resort, proved effective in increasing the children's attention span and making it possible for them to focus on personal and educational activities. Some parents have documented how Ritalin absolutely turned their children's lives around after nothing else had worked—they swear by it (e.g., Leavy, 1996).

In our reading, however, we have definitely been exposed to other perspectives. While we regard the vitriolic anti-Ritalin attacks of some individuals and groups as extreme, there is no denying that stimulants are drugs, and drugs have a downside. Many children seem to have very little trouble with Ritalin, but others exhibit side effects such as insomnia, stomach upset and abdominal pain, weight loss due to appetite suppression and changes in metabolic rate, irritability, mood swings, headaches, dizziness, and allergic reactions. Frequently, these reactions are mild and of short duration, diminishing after a week or two. Sometimes, too, they're due not to Ritalin, but to something else. Monitoring and adjusting the dosage often reduces or eliminates the problems.

Be that as it may, such side effects are worrisome, especially when it's your own child in question. And what about the other "stuff"? While it's difficult to determine facts and sort out cause and effect, toxic psychotic episodes have been reported by some—complete with hallucinations. Rebound effects have also been noted, where behavior worsens dramatically as children "come down" from the meds in the afternoon and evening. However, since these episodes are hard to measure, it's difficult to know what's truly occurring. Some investigators, concerned about weight loss and other side effects, recommend drug holidays. (It's felt that these are short-term, transient effects, but some professionals contend that the jury is still out on the matter.) Others, in the absence of longitudinal studies on the medical effects of long-term usage, worry that stimulants may place individuals at risk for later cardiovascular or related problems. As well, there is some evidence to suggest that, in very rare cases, a few Ritalin users might develop tics. For others, existing tics may be exacerbated. Importantly, should worse come to worst, one can simply stop taking medication if problems develop. Since Ritalin's shelf life is so short and it passes quickly from the body, the side effects generally disappear rapidly once it is discontinued. And although many parents are concerned about long-term substance abuse, certain studies have shown no association between taking stimulant medication in childhood and drug involvement later in life. In fact, quite the opposite has been found in some cases, where the use of stimulant medication has given young people a healthy respect for the consequences of drug usage and actually reduced their risk of moving on to "harder" substances (Chilcoat & Breslau, 1999; Weiss & Hechtman, 1993).

As mentioned earlier, some kids do not respond to stimulant medication: it's an ineffective alternative for them. Others "overspend" and end up in a zombie-like stupor (which can often be dealt with by changing the dose). A small number of ADHD children simply cannot tolerate any stimulants at all.

To complicate matters further, some educators question the existence of the disorder itself (Armstrong, 1996). Whose needs are being met? Could it be those of drug manufacturers, medical practitioners, and ineffective parents and teachers? Are we abdicating parental and pedagogical responsibilities by creating, or at least over diagnosing, ADHD? As Hancock (1996) suggested, has Ritalin (in some homes) taken the place of time with the child, and become "mother's little helper"? It can certainly be a time saver. Do so many children really need medication to function? How did so many children cope without it before? Does prescribing Ritalin sometimes absolve the child from responsibility and take others off the hook as well? Is ADHD becoming a desired diagnosis? (Smelter, Rasch, Fleming, Nazos, & Baranowski, 1996). Some parents we've worked with certainly treat it almost as a status symbol.

It makes sense to us to consider all points of view, and at least hear the voices of those who have reacted negatively toward the ADHD "industry" and the entrenchment of Ritalin as an automatic treatment (Block, 1996; Breggin, 1998; DeGrandpre, 1999; Diller, 1998; Nylund, 2000; Stein, 1999; Walker III, 1998). Many of the above writers are speaking out against the "hyperactivity hoax" and the "myth of ADHD", challenging the dopamine deficiency hypothesis, and suggesting that attention deficit is a culturally manufactured disorder. In their opinion, we are accepting unproven speculation and "blaming" children's brains instead of addressing the real causes. Ritalin and other stimulants, in their view, may simply mask problems by stimulating the central nervous system. They also often observe that many studies supporting the use of medication have been funded by the major drug manufacturers themselves (who obviously have a vested interest in the research outcomes).

DeGrandpre (1999) has wondered if, in an effort to cope with today's fast-paced society, we haven't created "generation Rx". He sees Ritalin as potentially addictive, and points out it is powerful and dangerous when crushed and snorted. Nylund (2000) has asked whether we might, with our current overreliance on drugs, be indiscriminately medicating our Huckleberry Finns. It does give one pause when, according to Breggin (1998, p. 99), even the firm producing the drug has cautioned: "Sufficient data on safety and efficacy of long-term use of Ritalin are not yet available."

Many of the concerns may be exaggerated. Although it is commonly accepted that stimulant usage among school children is increasing by leaps and bounds across America, some studies have found that ADHD is not overdiagnosed and that Ritalin is not overprescribed (cf. Weyandt, 2001). Other literature indicates otherwise, however, and shows that rates of stimulant medication treatment are clearly on the rise in the United States (Safer & Krager, 1994). Material we've read certainly suggests this is the case in Canada (Sheppard, 1998).

Looking at the big picture, we must admit that we're not entirely comfortable with the current state of affairs, especially when even some of the "big names" in the area have indicated that long-term effects of stimulant medication have not been well studied. As parents, we had some real concerns about side effects: we were, after all, talking about our own daughter.

Certain medical practitioners we know seem to think that Ritalin is the be-all and end-all in the treatment of ADHD. Conversely, some lobbying groups feel it is evil, dangerous, and to be avoided at all costs. As usual, we expect that the truth is somewhere in between. Reasoned professionals understand that Ritalin isn't for everybody, that it must be carefully monitored, and that it shouldn't be used in isolation (Barkley, 1998). It appears to help many ADHDers quickly, effectively, and safely, with a minimum of side effects. By using medication with respect, monitoring carefully, adjusting dosage appropriately, and striking a balance between it and other treatments, many problems can be avoided (Fachin, 1996; Hancock, 1996; Thompson, 1996; Whalen & Henker, 1991).

Since reactions differ from person to person, Melmed (2001) and others have advocated taking an extremely flexible approach to stimulants and treatment in general. Types of drugs, dosage, and optimal time of administration will vary depending upon the individual and the situation. For some, medication is best taken in the morning; for others it might do the most good just before bedtime. And because we don't have the same executive function challenges every day, it might be advisable for certain ADHDers to take their meds twice on some days, once on others, and not at all on others. The short shelf life of Ritalin, for example, means that it is virtually discontinued every day anyway, so flexibility in its administration is very much an option. In sum, the same rules for treatment must not be automatically applied to everyone: the personal and social context should be examined in each instance.

There are many factors to be considered. We've seen an extreme case where things were so horrible something had to be done; the child's life and the lives of those around him were not worth living. Medication was the last hope. With many other youngsters, the situation wasn't quite so desperate, but Ritalin was still a sensible and useful alternative that had positive outcomes. On the other hand, there are times we feel that parents, not the child, have the need for an ADHD label and medication. Unfortunately, we've also seen many situations where parents want Ritalin as an easy way out, and they get it effortlessly.

We stand in the middle on the issue—not diametrically opposed to medication, but not wildly enthusiastic either. Ideally, stimulants should be prescribed and monitored carefully, and there should be ongoing communication with parents and school personnel. However, the world being what it is, a lot of people seem to be falling short of the ideal a lot of the time. There is, we believe, significant overuse and abuse.

In Amber's case, we decided to try to cope without giving her medication. Ritalin was prescribed early just before she entered school. However, after a short trial (where she quieted down, but lost much of her pizzazz), we took her off. For better or for worse, we wanted Amber to be Amber! Her animation was a strength to be cherished and nurtured, not suppressed. As well, there was a fundamental principle at stake: we didn't want our girl to get the idea that her behavior was the result of a magic pill. We preferred that she gradually try to handle things by developing internal controls, exercising responsibility, and taking ownership for her actions. Of course, there were many to support her in the process. Interestingly, in one Canadian study, a number of "normal" adults who had reportedly "outgrown" their childhood hyperactivity did not usually credit drug treatment for their success. Rather, they pointed to a significant adult in their lives who believed in and supported them (Schwarzbeck, 1994). Most longitudinal research has failed to uncover any difference between those ADHDers who had been medicated earlier in their lives and those who had not (Weiss & Hechtman, 1993).

About five or six years ago, Amber actually asked to try Ritalin again to help her concentrate, study, and get through her academic upgrading. Although her concentration did improve, she wasn't thrilled with how the drug made her feel. This time around, like many others who start medication in late adolescence or early adulthood, she felt uncomfortable and quickly took herself off. Others noticed the effects of the Ritalin trial as well. Corey, Amber's then fiancé, now husband, stopped the car to ask: "What's the matter with you? You've listened to me speak for 30 minutes straight!" That had never happened before. And Chris queried: "What's wrong? Have you been smoking whacky tabaccy?" Amber and her family have grown to like who she is, and don't want that interfered with.

For parents considering medication for their children, we'd suggest being very certain about the diagnosis. All too often, a label of ADHD is slapped on youngsters prematurely, before anyone has taken a good long look at all the circumstances. With so many different perspectives out there and so much contradictory literature, it's hard to know what to believe. When unsure, it seems prudent to take the road of caution. Many treatment options ought to be explored. Rather than being the first and only resort, medication should always be used in combination with other interventions (sometimes to make them possible). Involve many parties in diagnosis and treatment. Make sure you have a conscientious doctor who monitors the situation regularly and who communicates with the school. Initially, make many visits to the physician and school to keep on top of the situation. If things go well, wonderful, but continue to do updates every now and again.

Several doctors of our acquaintance feel that ADHD is a lifelong disorder, and that stimulant medication should, therefore, be a lifelong affair. We're not so sure. It doesn't make sense to us to maintain the status quo without reevaluating the situation on an ongoing basis. If children improve so that other treatments have an impact, perhaps they can be weaned from the meds. Don't do anything precipitous here, but always keep abreast of the situation.

Diet

During the last twenty years or so, many diets have been proposed that supposedly "cure" hyperactivity. The most well-known of these was developed by Feingold (1975), but there have been many variations upon the original theme. Literature abounds, both pro and con (Conners, 1980; Crook, 1977; Greenberg & Horn, 1991; Ingersoll, 1988; Martin, Welsh, McKay, & Bareuther, 1984; Moghadam, 1988; Oud, 1988; Wender, 1987).

Basically, elimination diets involve abstaining as much as possible from foods containing additives such as dyes, salicylates, preservatives, and artificial flavoring. Many also try to eliminate "suspect foods", including those high in refined carbohydrates and sugar. Feingold (1975) himself, theorizing that hyperactivity is caused by a reaction to food additives, believed that as many as half of overactive children developed their problems due to their diets. Of course, we are what we eat; it is obviously important to have a healthy diet. Some children do react to specific substances. And some researchers feel 15% or so of ADHD children improve if refined sugar is controlled in the diet (since sugar can trigger a pancreatic reaction, a shift in blood sugar level, and attentional and hyperactive symptoms).

Despite the popularity of this approach (people looking for a magic solution again), most rigorous studies do not support it. At best, the literature is extremely equivocal. Logic compels us to ask, if such diets work so wonderfully, why do we have all these overactive kids running around? We should have been able to cure the condition by now.

Although a small number of ADHDers, those sensitive to additives and other substances, may respond positively to dietary restrictions and modifications (Schmidt, Mocks, Lay, Eisert, Fojkar, Fritz-Sigmund, Marcus, & Musaeus, 1997), the bulk of the research shows that removing sugar (or aspartame) from the diet does not result in improved behavior or attention in most hyperactive children (cf. Barkley, 1998; Goldstein & Goldstein, 1998; Weyandt, 2001).

At this stage, we're highly skeptical of the heavy-duty diet crazes. For one thing, they're extremely difficult to follow—one would have to be a farm-owning dietitian to have a chance. To illustrate, of the hundreds of preservatives available and in use, only a small fraction are ever listed on food labels. Aside from being impractical, diets that attempt to weed out dairy products and carbohydrates may actually do harm.

Further, even though some parents and medical personnel swear by the Feingold diet or similar approaches, there are alternative explanations for much of the diet-supporting research. Because these diets are really quite restrictive, they affect and literally change the lifestyle of hyperactive children and their families. Along with the diet itself, there is a change in routine (which often involves explaining the diet to the children, shopping with them, cooking together, and strict scheduling of meals). Many have suggested, then, that it's not the diet itself, but the resulting change in lifestyle that produces the desired effect. And therein may lie at least part of the answer—more time with the child, more structure, and more organization in the home.

It's important to be cautious here—all the data are not yet in. A few of the newer studies provide a degree of support for allergy-elimination diets and the possibility that food additives may play some role in attention deficit (cf. Goldstein & Goldstein, 1998; Schmidt, Mocks, Lay, Eisert, Fojkar, Fritz-Sigmund, Marcus, & Musaeus, 1997). As it stands now, though, it is premature to rush headlong into diets that likely have limited worth. If restrictive diets are ever found to have their place, it will be in combination with other treatments—they will not generally be cure-alls in and of themselves.

While elimination diets assume that certain additives or substances are causing attentional and related problems, nutritional supplement approaches are based on the notion that something is missing from the diet of ADHDers. To correct this shortage, as it were, supplements are recommended, including amino acids, glyconutrients, megavitamins, minerals, and phytonutrients. According to a few studies using parent ratings, supplements have decreased the ADHD symptoms of some children. However, for the most part, research has not been particularly supportive, and most pro-supplement studies have been poorly designed (Dykman & Dykman, 1998). More work is obviously required.

The danger is that diet fads are intuitively appealing—they offer a relatively easy way out. Too many desperate parents grasp at this possibility unthinkingly and ignore other potential options. We wouldn't dismiss the elimination diet and nutritional supplement alternatives out-of-hand, but we do view them very, very cautiously. For us, it's simply "not that big a deal". If children are reacting to certain foods and substances or missing something in their diet, it isn't that difficult for parents to monitor, control, and improve the quality of food intake. And it can usually be done without turning family routines upside down. In Amber's case, we simply watched her eating habits, particularly around holidays such as Easter, Halloween, and Christmas.

Modified Behavior Modification

Frequently, the time-honored behavior modification approach is recommended as a possible solution for attention deficit. However, all too often, people talk about putting a behavior mod. program into place without really understanding the complexity of the issues and what it really means. Behavior modification isn't simply giving a child M & M's for being good; the process is much more involved than that.*

Many years ago, we had a mother come in and announce proudly to us that she had put her overactive child on a behavior mod. program. Knowing the mother, we were skeptical, with good reason as it turned out. She went on to say that she was using positive reinforcers to encourage proper behavior on the part of her youngster. When we asked what the reinforcers were, we found that the first time the child was "good", he received a watch, the second time a camera, and the third time a snowmobile. This program wasn't going to work—behavior modification has to be more than simple bribery. In this case, it was clear the mother was soon going to run out of tempting reinforcers; a Cadillac would have had to be next.

Generally, we're not as fond of behavior modification approaches as many other investigators, for—having worked in a real school district with real people—we understand the difficulty of putting such programs into place. We acknowledge that behavior modification can be extremely effective in some situations, particularly when dealing with captive audiences (such as mentally-challenged youngsters in institutions). We also accept the efficacy of such programs in other settings, but it is important to realize that a great deal of energy and time are required to run them efficiently. If appropriate supports and resources are available, behavior modification is an excellent option in some situations. However,

---

*For an excellent description of what behavior modification is and how to do it, see Martin and Pear (1998).

to be effective, it must be done systematically, not in a haphazard fashion. And remember, ADHDers aren't easy to reach, whatever the approach.

In an effort to illustrate quickly some principles of behavior modification, we'll deal with two examples together. The first involves a young kindergarten student we worked with more than two decades ago; the second refers to some of the classic experimentation done with pigeons. Obviously, we feel our real-life, human example is more relevant to the discussion at hand, but birds are easier.

Starting with our feathered friends first, we marvel that B. F. Skinner accomplished the amazing feat of teaching pigeons to play Ping-Pong. Here, let's content ourselves with a simpler question: How did Skinner and others get pigeons (housed in a Skinner box) to learn to peck a disk? The answer: they used the principle of reward or positive reinforcement to shape each bird's behavior. Things were wired up electronically: at first the pigeon automatically received a food pellet each time it pecked the disk. That is, every peck yielded a juicy morsel—reinforcement was immediate. At this juncture, behavior modifiers have what they term a continuous schedule of reinforcement—every single time the bird makes the desired or correct response, it is reinforced.

While such a continuous schedule is effective in maintaining behavior, it would be impossible to implement over the long term in the real world. Quite simply, one can't reinforce each and every appropriate response made by a child or an animal. As a consequence, it is necessary to move on to other schedules. One possibility is a FR (fixed ratio) schedule, where reinforcement takes place after a set number of responses. For example, a pigeon on a FR schedule might be rewarded with a food pellet every 10th time it makes the correct pecking response. Fixed schedules do maintain behavior—think of your regular paycheck, your night out, or watching Sunday football.

Another option is to move gradually or directly to a VR (variable ratio) schedule, an even more powerful reinforcement mechanism, where the bird never knows for sure when the reward is coming. On some occasions, it will occur after every pecking response, on others after the 5th, or the 10th, or the 99th, or the 1022nd, or whenever. Incidentally, if units of time are being used (say reinforcement is administered every 10 minutes, or at varying time periods), the reinforcement schedule is known as FI or VI (Fixed or Variable Interval).

Behavior modifiers tell us, quite accurately, that variable ratio or interval schedules are the most powerful ones for maintaining animal and human behavior. There are many examples. In our last home, on River Road, we were afforded the constant spectacle of fisherpeople casting their lines in the water just across the way. It was amazing to us, for many of these individuals seemed never to catch anything, yet they'd return day after day after day. You can tell we're biased, but it seemed like such a colossal waste of time and effort to us. Yet every now and again, they'd catch a fish, and the infrequent successes kept them coming back through the entire fishing season. A classic variable schedule! Another, of course, is gambling. With bingo, slot machines, or other games of chance, we never know when the reinforcement is coming (but we all know how addictive they can be). It might be a coincidence, but deep down we believe that the designer of the TicTac mints package was an apt student of behavior modification. One can jiggle those candies for quite a while without getting any. Then suddenly, and you never know quite when, several come pouring out—a variable schedule par excellence.

Let's move to our more human example; the little nipper who came to kindergarten and created virtual havoc. The kindergarten teacher at the time made out the shortest referral we've ever received: it just said "Help!" Later, in conversation with us, she indicated, in flat despair, that this hyper youngster was "never in his seat". She had tried to work out a plan with the parents, but nothing was going well. The parents were tremendously sincere and well-intentioned, but the boy, who was adopted, had been a victim of rather horrific early abuse that had left its mark. Although everyone tried their best to provide support, the young fellow was quite literally "wild".

To say that a child is "never in his seat" isn't enough for a real behavior modifier; we had to gather accurate data and establish firm baselines. Ergo, armed with a trusty stopwatch, the first author observed and recorded this boy's behavior for 15 minutes on two separate occasions. And when all the timing was done, it was found that the teacher's observations weren't quite correct; the boy was "almost never in his seat" (he remained seated for less than a minute during each observation). Our target was clear, then; the first goal was to get his rear end in the chair. We felt that once we had him a little more settled, other aspects of programming could be put into place. The program itself wasn't difficult to design, but it took a fair amount of personpower. For one thing, an extra pair of hands was required in the classroom to monitor the boy's behavior carefully, and to administer rewards immediately. The principle of immediate reinforcement is central to behavior modification. Young children don't really understand deferred gratification; if they do something good, they want their reward now. By the by, although we're not opposed to a treat once in a while, overusing food for reinforcement can cause eating disorders (Kennedy, Terdal, & Fusetti, 1993).

With this little guy, we opted to go with poker chips. Plenty of research has been done with using token economies (almost a monetary system of reward), and it worked here. The poker chips seemed to be intrinsically rewarding in their own right—the kid liked them. However, in an attempt to build in some long-term consequences and involve the parents as the good guys in the process, we also allowed the youngster to earn a bonus. Specifically, if he sat still long enough and accumulated a certain number of tokens over the course of the week, his parents would take him for a Saturday outing—and he loved those. In essence, then, we went through the same process as behavior modifiers do with pigeons. Initially, the boy received a token every time he sat in his desk for a few moments. Gradually, though, we moved to a fixed ratio schedule, where he was reinforced every 5th time he sat down. And eventually, we got to the variable ratio stage. The approach worked rather well. Although the boy remained fidgety, overactive, and on the move for much of the day, he certainly began to stay put for far longer periods than he had at the outset. A beginning had been made.

In the long run, we must strive to move beyond concrete reinforcers. Tangible rewards are nice, but we also want youngsters to internalize values and try to behave because it's the "right" thing to do. Social reinforcers—attention, praise, and eventually internal self-satisfaction—are the ultimate.

Setting up behavior mod. programs for ADHD kids is not quite the same as doing it for "regular" children (thus, the "modified behavior modification" heading to this section). With most students, the goal is to move systematically from continuous through to other schedules. At that point, for many, the job is done. The children internalize the idea and the main aim has been accomplished. However, because they tend to be "inconsequential" (have trouble linking cause and effect), impulsive, and inattentive, ADHDers are sometimes different in this respect. Since they don't focus, they miss things along the way, and often forget even after they've been through the process several times. It can become an ongoing cycle, where one must take ADHD kids from continuous to fixed or variable schedules, and then go back repeatedly and start the process all over again. These children often require an abnormal amount of continuous, concrete reinforcement.

As indicated earlier, Amber liked her stickers. Some teachers picked up on this interest, and offered her stickers as tangible rewards for staying on task. Perhaps because she experienced so little success in school, Amber sometimes responded positively to this type of reinforcement (and to behavioral charts, graphs, and so on). By forcing them to watch her closely (to administer the reinforcement), such methods encouraged the adults to look for positives and "catch her doing it right". The use of concrete reinforcers such as stickers or stars has been shown to be beneficial for hyperactive children. Not only do such positive reinforcers encourage task completion, they also reward youngsters for not disturbing others. In this, the age of technology, it makes sense to use "time on the computer" as a reinforcer as well. Because of the entertainment value and stimulating graphics, many ADHDers, including Amber, stick to task on a computer better than on anything else. When this is the case, it's important to take advantage of the opportunity. Good CD-ROM and educational software programs, with built-in, immediate-reward systems, can be incredibly motivating.

Behavioral contracts have also proven effective with Amber and others. These formal documents (you can turn the signing ceremony into quite an occasion) spell out expected behavior, highlight its importance, and specify the roles and duties of parents, teachers, and the child. Of course, one often hears the complaint, "We tried using contracts (or behavior modification, or whatever), but it didn't work." Sometimes it may be true, but all too often we find one of two things: that people don't give these methods a fair chance, or that they grab on desperately and overuse them. Naturally, children become bored and less responsive if contracts, for example, are overexposed and worked to death. However, at the right place and time, a thoughtfully designed contract can be a powerful tool. If it works for a while, well and good. Then, a few months later, it might pay to resurrect the approach once more.

Some parents with a behavioral bent try to control overactive behavior by implementing very structured, firm schedules for their children. For example, they'll have a 15 minute milk-and-cookie break for them the moment they arrive home from school, then allow a half hour to play ball, then bring them in for a half hour of homework, then have 45 minutes for supper, then a half hour for music practice, then 15 minutes of play, 15 minutes of reading, an hour of television, and bed. In Amber's case, we opted not to go with such a regimented, military-like schedule. On occasion, we found it beneficial to be structured—we sometimes had to be highly regimented indeed to get her to accomplish basic tasks. On balance, though, we felt that overdoing this sort of heavy-handed approach would almost have destroyed her childhood—Amber wasn't built for the army, and neither were we. While we see the advantages of tight scheduling for some situations, we generally prefer a malleable approach (with firm input when required).

Consistent Structure/Discipline

It has been said that ADHDers need discipline like all kids, only more so. Some adults, in an effort to add structure, tend to write down rigid routines, post them with magnets on the fridge door, and hold their offspring to "the rules" with a vengeance. While a certain amount of structure of this type can be positive (What kid doesn't need routines at some time?), overdoing it can cause problems. We're not raising automatons, but children. Good parents and teachers remember what it was like to be a child (McCluskey, 2000b): they recall the doubts, the fears, and the joys. When our daughter is looking back on her childhood and youth, we want her to remember spontaneous, happy times, not schedules.

Having said that, we accept the need for some degree of structure when dealing with overactive kids. Perhaps above all else, one needs a plan. It's amazing how many parents and teachers, frustrated by hyperactive children, have no firm plan in place for dealing with them. We are reminded of Socrates' famous comment, "If a man does not know to what port he is sailing, no wind is favorable." As we've said, sometimes Amber's antics were so bizarre that, plan as we might, it was impossible to predict her behavior or our response. Still, even on these occasions, we had a plan of sorts in place—we'd stall! Assuming we weren't in time-out mode (that's to be handled differently), we would simply escort Amber to a secure setting (usually a bedroom) for safekeeping, and hold a parental summit meeting to come up with an original response for an original event. Many theorists have emphasized the need for having a plan in dealing with misbehavior (Glasser, 1978), and we agree. If you float along aimlessly with an overactive youngster, it'll soon be a case of the tail wagging the dog. Parents must take charge, know where they're going, and set appropriate expectations (Barkley, 2000).

There is plenty of evidence to suggest that ADHD children need predictable routines—sudden changes can really "get them going". At home, there is often acting out when parents leave and others, less familiar with the child, take over. It can be hard getting babysitters for ADHDers. We know—we had to pay triple! It almost becomes a Calvin and Hobbes scenario. (While almost everyone else found this comic strip hilarious, some parents of hyperactive children definitely didn't. It struck too close to home.) In school there is a parallel—the substitute. Subs can be driven to distraction (and from the school) by ADHD kids whose routines have been disrupted. To prevent this sort of thing from happening, careful planning is required.

Both at home and at school, we recognize the need for firmness in dealing with Amber and other hyperactive children. We're not talking about rigid, arbitrary rules that are stifling and cruel, but rather wise use of structure and organization. As parents, we came down hard on safety issues (such as hiding in the oven or gallivanting on hydro wires). We also took a dim view of disrespectful behavior. Amber might misbehave, but we felt she had the ability to treat her parents, teachers, adults, and other kids with respect. As we confessed earlier, we never believed in spanking until Amber came along. However, there truly was a need to stop her from doing dangerous things. What would you do if your child, despite repeated warnings and discussions, persisted in riding her bike into the street without looking, swimming in hazardous waters, and running on top of monkey bars? In general, we still don't believe in corporal punishment, for we think it models aggression. With Amber, though, there had to be (forgive us the pun) a bottom line. In truth, we often felt like beating her, but we held back and confined ourselves to administering the occasional swat on the behind. It was important for her to know that spanking was in our repertoire and that she couldn't push things too far.

Although it's often tempting to resort to physical punishment with kids, it generally isn't all that effective. Many educators see "punishment" as an inadequate, reactive response because it imposes consequences arbitrarily, emphasizes blind obedience, and relies primarily on force. They prefer proactive "discipline", since it focuses on developing internal controls (Brendtro, Brokenleg, & Van Bockern, 1990). With impulsive ADHDers, who so often fail to link cause and effect, punishment may be particularly ineffective. (If they don't associate punishment directly with their misbehavior, why would it have any impact?) Some theorists go so far as to argue that many of these youngsters take corporal punishment in their stride due to a lack of "pain filters": once they get all wound up, it's difficult to stop or physically hurt them. For us, it's simply that modeling aggression is generally undesirable—it should not be done lightly.

Phelan (1991), recognizing that we often negotiate and talk too much when dealing with misbehaving children, offered his popular *1-2-3 Magic* approach to help keep parents and educators on track. This simple strategy reduces words to a minimum. When preschool and preteen children act up, Phelan's advice is simply for the adult on the scene to hold up an index finger and say "That's 1". Should the misbehavior continue after the initial warning, two raised fingers accompany the words "That's 2". Two warnings are deemed to be enough. If there is a third incident, three fingers go up to emphasize the final statement, "That's 3, take 5". By keeping verbiage to a minimum, adults using this technique avoid getting into arguments or power struggles with youngsters. After strike three, children are "escorted" to their rooms for a brief time-out. With adolescents, fines or some other method can be employed.

At school, hyperactive students need all sorts of supervision. Remember the earlier example; simply sending an ADHD child out on the playground (to burn off energy) without a watchful adult on hand is setting the stage for disaster. In the classroom, some educators believe it is almost impossible to overstructure the environment for hyperactive youngsters. In their view, externally imposed routines and rules will eventually help these children develop their own internal controls. We're dubious about this sort of approach: to our minds, it's definitely possible to overstructure a hyper child's life to the point of making him or her miserable.

However, solid structure, if employed sensibly and compassionately, can be helpful. Charts and graphs are effective tools in setting routines and helping the child see progress. It is usually not wise, though, to use charts to compare hyperactive children to others in the class; it is often better to have separate records for them alone. When active children reach a major goal on the chart, they can take it home to "show off" to their parents. Formal time-outs, in separate locations or rooms, can also be used, or ADHD kids can "cool off" by putting their heads down on their desks for a while or moving to an isolated corner in the back of the room. ADHDers should not be singled out for an endless barrage of punishment; consequences and opportunities should be distributed among all the students.

Almost all writers in the parenting realm emphasize the need for consistency. Going back to the work of Bateson and his colleagues in the '50s, a case can certainly be made for being consistent with children. In their early double-bind hypothesis, it was suggested that an excess of inconsistent, double-binding communication (notably from mother to child) could cause schizophrenia (Bateson, Jackson, Haley, & Weakland, 1956).

In a double-bind communication, the verbal and nonverbal elements of the message are contradictory. A classic, not-so-apocryphal example involves an overprotective mother, who tells her young son with a school phobia: "I know you won't be afraid of school any more, Johnny." She has said the right thing, but—if the statement is accompanied by tears, a sobbing tone of voice, a tense facial expression, and desperate hand-wringing—she is communicating quite the opposite nonverbally. While it is extreme and inaccurate to say that such double-binds cause schizophrenia per se, there is some good evidence to suggest that these kinds of communications are disturbing to many children (McCluskey & Albas, 1981). Young children, in particular, can be confused by inconsistent, incongruent messages of this type. Although older youngsters frequently understand sarcasm (and the tone that belies the words), young children tend to zero in on the words alone; negative words may be interpreted simply as negative, without regard to positive tone or humorous intent. In fact, it has even been suggested that teachers who rely heavily on sarcasm should not be placed in the early primary grades.

With hyperactive youngsters, it's a struggle to remain consistent, but it's also very important. No matter how patient you are, it's easy to fall into the trap of reacting too angrily to the behavior of an ADHD child. Then, after calming down and feeling guilty, there's a tendency to overcompensate by being too lenient. These sorts of ups and downs lead to confusion and should be avoided wherever possible. Of course, since we're all human, some negative incidents are to be expected. Overall, however, parents should strive for an even, consistent style.

There is also the danger of inconsistency between parents. In the typical paradigm, the father might emerge as the tough disciplinarian while the mother, to compensate, spends a lot of time "loving up" the child and, in essence, giving the youngster anything he or she wants. This is a mistake. Such inconsistency can cause more trouble than enough. If parents see such a pattern emerging, they should take steps to make changes. Although the father may always remain assertive and directive, he might learn to relax the rules a bit, soften the cumbrous atmosphere, and enjoy his child. And while the mother might always remain the more lenient of the two, she could learn to take a somewhat more firm approach. Lighten up and tighten up respectively. By supporting each other, communicating, and working together to send consistent messages to the child, parents can accomplish a great deal.

The "TEAM" approach suggests that parents can consistently use four strategies to address behavioral problems of hyperactive young people (Stevens & McCluskey, 1998). The strategies are: talk (to communicate, listen, involve the children in planning and doing, ascertain their point of view, and share your reactions and suggestions); experiences (to capture and hold children's interest and encourage responsible actions through logical consequences); approval (to provide positive feedback, reinforcement, and success experiences); and modeling (to show children appropriate behavior on an ongoing basis: youngsters learn from and imitate what they see, so parents must behave well themselves).

We think modeling is especially critical. Parents who want to set a good example must avoid the "do-as-I-say-not-as-I-do" trap. Children, often unconsciously, copy adults—smokers, drinkers, and drug users really shouldn't be all that shocked when their offspring end up smoking, drinking, and doing drugs. And angry, aggressive parents are quite apt to raise angry, aggressive kids. A long time ago, a co-worker shared a story that has stuck with us. Apparently, his preschool daughter loved to sit beside him in the car and pretend to drive the vehicle. One day, as she was busily engrossed in this activity, she stuck her head out the window and screamed at a surprised motorist: "Get out of the way, you stupid ass!" It was clearly time for someone to begin more positive modeling.

To prevent the child from playing both ends against the middle, expectations should be similar across settings. Communication is essential between home and school and within the school (where the principal should get together with all teachers involved with the ADHD child). From class to class and teacher to teacher, behavioral expectations and discipline should be consistent.

Time-Out

One of the most popular and effective techniques for some ADHD children is the "time-out" (Clark, 1989). But using time-out to good effect can be a challenging procedure requiring planning and thought. Some of us send children to their rooms to curb bad behavior, but in so doing we're sometimes subtly reinforcing it. Look at a typical child's room of today, complete with toys, television, VHS or DVD, CD player, and video game system. Not a bad place to be! In fact, too good a place if we want to address, not reward, inappropriate behavior. While we aren't suggesting banishing children to a Spartan dungeon or torture chamber, a time-out area should be rather sparse, boring, and dull—not uncomfortable, but not palatial either. Parents might provide a cozy chair to curl up in, without throwing in all of the amenities. When Amber was placed in a time-out setting, Chris and any other kids on hand were asked to play elsewhere for a few minutes: the "time-outee" is to be left alone for a spell. We also had to remove all pets, for being with them would definitely have been a reward as far as Amber was concerned.

It has been suggested not to place a child in time-out for longer than one minute for each year of age (Clark, 1989). Not a bad guideline. Certainly, time-outs should be short: don't send children "up for life" or abandon them for hours on end. Setting up an area close at hand is important: the idea is to get there quickly, not have time-outs across town at Gramma's house. If available, an extra room is a good possibility, or even a corner of an infrequently used room (which can be "insulated" by using dividers and placing a chair facing the wall). The idea, however, is not to embarrass children by putting them on public display, but rather to give them time to reflect. For safety reasons, if time-out is used with very young children, they should be kept in view.

Time-out worked well with Amber in many instances. For one thing, because she'd get all wound up and frantic, it gave her a chance to calm down and think for a bit. Following Glasser's (1978) lead, we'd put her in a time-out area to "work it out" (which she usually did before the allotted "release time"). Once Amber settled down enough to control herself and discuss things, the time-out was ended. We took pains to explain the reason for time-outs before we implemented them, and debriefed after each one. In a sense, time-outs allowed Amber to make a fresh start after bad episodes, but she had to earn that privilege by behaving calmly and rationally. Like anything else, we wouldn't want to work time-out to death by using it too frequently, but, employed in a balanced way, it can become a very effective tool in the parental arsenal.

Communication and Social Skills

Good communication is, of course, a two-way street. Adults should take pains to ensure that young hyperactive children receive and understand the messages being sent. In some of the work on compliance training, information is provided to help parents give more effective directions to ADHDers (Greenberg & Horn, 1991). Among other things, it is suggested that adults (1) be specific; (2) give instructions one at a time (i.e., avoid "chain commands"); (3) use mostly "go", as opposed to "stop" commands; and (4) "tell", rather than "ask".

Amber, when she was younger, tended to respond best to short, specific, one-or two-step instructions. If flooded with too many directions, she'd be overwhelmed. Like other ADHDers, Amber usually couldn't pay attention long enough to listen and remember the instructions. And even if she did, she couldn't stay on task long enough to carry them out; she'd get distracted in the middle and fly off to something else. As a consequence, we kept directions very basic. Precise, short tasks worked better than multi-step impossible dreams.

Direct verbal cues served as a form of reality check for Amber. We might say very clearly to her, "You're being a nuisance. We expect you to sit still now." We'd definitely "call" her on bad behavior. Borrowing from Glasser (1978) again, we'd interrupt Amber's inappropriate actions by asking "What are you doing?" This approach was especially effective when her friends were around. By simply asking the question in that way, it put the onus back on Amber, and forced her to explain and take some responsibility for her behavior. It also let her know that we'd had enough:

if she didn't shape up, there would be other consequences. On many occasions, Amber refocused, thought about what she was doing, and made adjustments.

As Amber got older, we were able to talk to her about her attentional problems. We agreed that we would try to give subtle verbal cues or signals without embarrassing or calling her on the carpet. One of our favorite words was *derang*. When we saw Amber beginning to get overly "rangy", we'd simply whisper "derang" in her direction. If she didn't cease and desist, we'd repeat it with more force. Very often, this verbal cue was enough to settle her down. At other times, we'd treat overactivity lightly at first, by saying pleasantly, "You're getting too antsy." Upon hearing those words, Amber would know it was time to back off. Sometimes she didn't, but we tried to give her a chance to de-escalate before using the heavy artillery.

In time, Amber started to give us considerable information about her state of mind. More and more, we could rely on her to clue us in. She'd talk, we'd listen. Amber can be quite a delight, and often her conversation is extremely edifying. As we've mentioned, she can be amazingly observant and insufferably pleased with herself when she makes intriguing observations. Why not take advantage of these skills by encouraging her to size up social situations, predict outcomes, and take the necessary action?

Hyperactive children and youth must learn not only to interpret messages from others, but also to communicate more effectively themselves. It's often a problem. As we've stressed, ADHDers—with their impulsive, disruptive, noisy, shrill, bossy, and intrusive style—can be a difficult burden for their peers and for adults.

Some professionals, speech/language pathologists in particular, have at their fingertips excellent programs to develop listening, speaking, and communication abilities. Many of these are useful for the ADHD child. Specific suggestions to improve listening and attention span are also offered in other sources (DeBruyn & Larson, 1984; Stevens & McCluskey, 1998). As well, social skills training curricula have been designed for at-risk young people (Connolly, Dowd, Criste, Nelson, & Tobias, 1995; Dowd & Tirney, 1992). Some, aimed directly at the ADHD population, help hyper individuals learn and apply appropriate social skills (Begun, 1995). Since the overall goal should be to teach responsibility, one wouldn't want to over focus on "cookbooky" lessons. Nevertheless, precise how-to-interact maps are a good starting point for many socially lost and isolated ADHDers.

Biofeedback/Self-Monitoring

Incidentally, this segment, as well as the following one on meta-cognition, could just as easily have been placed in the "indirect strategies" section. The goal of these techniques is to help children recognize, monitor, control, evaluate, and adjust their own behavior. In other words, the hope is that children gradually take charge, acquire their own internal standards and codes of behavior, and learn to act appropriately when adults are not at hand. At that point, since the adults aren't even there, the approaches might be considered to be indirect. However, we've opted to place both biofeedback and metacognition with "direct strategies", because both initially involve the direct teaching of skills from adult to child.

In their pure form, most common biofeedback techniques with ADHDers involve attaching electrodes to the scalp or elsewhere and measuring bodily activity (e.g., brain waves or muscle tension). The ADHD individuals, after being given feedback, then attempt to change their reactions (by altering brain activity, muscular response, or whatever). Although some clinicians believe biofeedback can decrease ADHD symptoms, a number of studies have failed to show that it is an effective treatment. On the other hand, several others have indicated that the technique might be useful with ADHD in some circumstances (Lubar, 1991; Potashkin & Beckles, 1990). At the moment, though, there is not really enough evidence to justify biofeedback as a primary treatment for the condition.

Taking a softer, less formal view of biofeedback, one goal for parents and educators might be to teach hyperactive children to recognize and interpret their own bodily cues. When overactive youngsters are involved in activities, their behavior frequently escalates out of control. Parents and teachers can help them recognize the signs that this is happening or about to happen. By learning to look for and identify signals such as feeling aggressive, shouting, yelling, pushing others, becoming flushed, and the like, ADHDers can make adjustments in an attempt to calm down and nip potential problems in the bud.

With hyperactive youngsters, then, the aim is to help them de-mystify the ADHD experience and grow more attuned to their physiological reactions and styles. The idea is that once children become aware of their own thoughts, feelings, and bodily reactions, they can become active participants in solving their motoric and attentional problems. Often, the intent is to get such youngsters to relax, slow down, and approach things in a more orderly, less impulsive manner. Self-monitoring is clearly the cornerstone of the entire process.

Valett (1974) has developed a number of exercises, including one called Slow Breathing, to help children focus on and adjust their physiological responses. In that particular exercise, the objective is to help youngsters relax by slowing down the number of breaths they take per minute. Overactive children are asked to relax, sit and breathe deeply, consciously inhale and exhale slowly, and count the number of breaths taken in a one-minute span. Gradually, they try to calm down and decrease the number of breaths taken per minute. To extend such activities, it has even been recommended that children use stethoscopes to listen to their heartbeats. Again, the goal is to count the beats per minute and, in an effort to relax, attempt to decrease them. A variety of similar exercises have been designed (Oud, 1988; Valett, 1974).

Valett presented many other activities for hyper students. One applies very much to Amber, albeit in reverse. As Valett noticed, many active youngsters eat too quickly; in their desire to be on to other things, they wolf down their food indiscriminately. To help them eat in unhurried fashion, Valett recommended that parents and ADHDers chart the behavior. The goal is to get the children to relax and take plenty of time while eating. Timing is done with a stopwatch and it is suggested that the kids take small bites. They are told to chew the food well, and taste it before swallowing. When they've finished eating, parents record what was eaten and how long it took. Next time, the aim is to take "even longer to eat".

In Amber's case, the opposite problem exists. She takes forever to eat anything. Because she is so distractible and distracting, Amber always bounces from one thing to another, so much so that she literally doesn't take time to eat. She's either talking (and disturbing others), or shifting her interest from activity to activity or to different objects in the room. In her situation, we have tried reversing the Valett activity to see if she can eat more quickly and finish meals with the rest of the family. It has been annoying in the past when everybody is done at mealtime, and Amber has barely started. This modified "fast eating" exercise helped Amber to recognize signs of distraction, think about remaining calm during meals, and adjust her eating rate.

In another of Valett's exercises (designed for seven or eight kids together), the goal is to whisper messages from child to child. Not only does this activity illustrate the mixups that can occur during communication (and how rumors get started), it also encourages overactive children to sit, listen, and speak in measured whispers without shouting impulsively. Again, one goal of the exercise is to get the youngsters to think about what they're doing during communication and monitor their voice levels.

Nowadays, with the availability of sophisticated physiological measurement apparatus and innovative computer programs, all sorts of biofeedback exercises are available, some in video game format. The basic principle remains the same, however: to help children become aware of, monitor, and control their physiological responses and behavior.

In some circles, the sensory integration approach has also become popular. Based on the notion that they are cursed with faulty arousal systems, sensory integration training (which is often quite costly) typically puts ADHDers through a series of exercises that supposedly stimulate and solidify nerve cell connections. The preponderance of well-designed research to date does not support such training as a treatment for ADHD (Ingersoll & Goldstein, 1993).

Metacognitive Strategies

To put it succinctly, metacognition means "thinking about thinking" (Armbruster & Brown, 1984; Elliott, Kratochwill, Cook, & Travers, 2000). Stating it another way, metacognitive knowledge is knowledge that allows us to reflect upon our thinking before, during, and after problem solving (Barrell, 1991). It seems intuitively obvious to us that all children, as much as possible, should learn to monitor their own thinking and behavior. By so doing, they can begin to make choices about their actions, rather than rely solely on directions from adults. By consciously monitoring their own cognitive strategies, children can become more in touch with their personal learning styles, strengths, and weaknesses.

Let's step back for a moment. Most of us talk about "parenting" as if the parents must take sole responsibility for the behavior of their children. This doesn't seem quite right; even in childhood individuals bear some of the responsibility for who they are and how they behave. From a metacognitive perspective, the term *childing* would be better, because it suggests that the job of parents is to help children take charge of their own behavior. Certainly, children should be encouraged to have some ownership for their own learning and conduct.

Flavell (1987) has stated that teachers should help learners acquire three types of metacognitive understanding. The first, "metacognitive self-knowledge", is a feeling for their strengths and weaknesses and how they learn best. Some children are good organizers, others are not; some possess good vocabularies, others do not; some have good memories, others do not; and some can concentrate well, while others cannot. Similarly, some children seem to learn best using visual cues, others prefer auditory ones, and still others (including many ADHDers) respond best to a hands-on, kinesthetic approach (Barbe & Petreshene, 1981; Dunn & Dunn, 1978; Dunn, Dunn, & Treffinger, 1992). If students know their strengths, they can highlight and work toward them; if they know their weaknesses, they can avoid or attempt to address them; and if they know their preferred learning style, they can structure situations and tasks to their best advantage. And teachers can adjust their styles depending on the strengths and weaknesses of the child. For example, a disorganized child who can't keep things straight might benefit from daybooks, homework sheets, and daily report cards.

The second of Flavell's skills is "task-metacognitive knowledge". Some children prefer true-false or multiple-choice questions, others like essays, and still others enjoy oral discussion (or even acting things out). They need to learn to study and organize themselves differently depending on the task: you do not prepare the same way for different types of tests or challenges.

The third skill is "knowledge of learning strategies". There are techniques to improve organizational, study, and problem-solving skills that can be taught even to young students. "Advance organizers", for example, can be used to help "prep" learners beforehand. When the lesson comes, they're ready. There are many other techniques to help students learn to study more effectively, including the well-known SQ3R (Survey, Question, Read, Recite, Review) approach (Robinson, 1972), and more recent variations thereof. And Creative Problem Solving or CPS (Isaksen, Dorval, & Treffinger, 2000; Treffinger, Isaksen, & Dorval, 2000) provides strategies for understanding problems and challenges, generating ideas, and preparing for action (including using creative and critical thinking, brainstorming, and a veritable toolbox of other skills).

Central to the topic at hand is that metacognitive training has been used to attempt to help ADHD kids think about what they're doing, understand their behavior, and gain some degree of self-control (Frank & Smith, 1994; Kendall & Braswell, 1985; Zentall & Meyer, 1987). Some researchers report positive results, and some educators indicate that teaching distractible students to use self-monitoring works very well in the classroom (Osborne, Kosiewicz, Crumley, & Lee, 1987). As indicated earlier, many contend that teaching social skills has also had positive impact on difficult students (Connolly, Dowd, Criste, Nelson, & Tobias, 1995; Dowd & Tierney, 1992; Forman, 1993; Stephens, 1992). On balance, however, although metacognitive training has helped many students build reading and other academic and organizational skills (Armbruster & Brown, 1984), Abikoff (1991), Ingersoll (1988), and others have found little evidence to suggest that it works well with hyperactive children.

Although much of the literature has been discouraging, we have some reason to believe that cognitive-behavioral training may well have a place in the treatment of ADHD. For one thing, we've been involved with one treatment facility for emotionally-fragile, behaviorally-disruptive children that serves many hyperactive children each year. Our experience there has been that Life Space Crisis Intervention or LSCI (Long, 1994; Long, Wood, & Fecser, 2001), a metacognitive strategy of sorts, has had a tangible impact on several ADHD students (Laferriere, Bastable, McCluskey, Anderson, & Torske, 1995; Bastable, Laferriere, & Kolodie, 1995). LSCI focuses the role of adults in guiding students through a problem-solving format, where conflict is seen as an opportunity rather than as a crisis. To summarize briefly, some of the therapeutic goals with LSCI are: (1) organizing reality: training students to perceive and interpret events accurately (i.e., to become aware of their own behavior and the reaction of others); (2) confronting unacceptable behavior: dealing directly with children who are very comfortable with their deviant behavior and receive gratification from it; (3) strengthening self-control: helping students who are burdened by remorse, shame, inadequacy, or guilt about their unworthiness; (4) teaching new social skills: assisting students who mean well, but lack the appropriate social behaviors; (5) exposing exploitation: supporting students who are being exploited by peers; and (6) red flagging: helping students who tend to overreact to normal rules and expectations (they often need assistance to identify the real reason for their behavior and ways to de-escalate it). Caregivers gain as well, for LSCI—along with other programs such as EQUIP (Gibbs, Potter, & Goldstein, 1995), Positive Peer Culture (Vorrath & Brendtro, 1985), and Resolving Conflict Creatively (Lantieri & Patti, 1996)—can teach them how to withdraw from the conflict cycle, react more empathically, and reframe crises and conflict into teaching and learning opportunities.

We don't see LSCI as a panacea, or even purely as a metacognitive technique. However, the approach has been effective for several ADHDers; they appear to learn to look for warning signs or "triggers", to attend to bodily cues, and to internalize strategies for more appropriate interaction with others. Staff at the center in question have also had success combining elements of LSCI and CPS. The Creative Learning Model (Treffinger, Isaksen, & Dorval, 1994) highlights the importance of working through three stages with students, where they first learn and use basic thinking "tools" (which are taught directly), then learn and practice CPS (in a safe, supportive setting with expert guidance), and finally work with real-life problems (and deal, more independently, with challenges that are encountered in everyday life).

One interesting metacognitive approach for hyperactive children is the Concentration Cockpit (Levine, 1987). In this "attention control system", Levine has designed (in cardboard format) an airplane-like cockpit, complete with various dials representing different aspects of behavior. There is a master control panel, and then adjacent dials to measure sensory filtration (not paying attention to irrelevant stimuli), free flight (not daydreaming), mood control, behavioral control, motor/verbal control, social control, memory control, and appetite control (not always wanting things, and looking ahead). Hyperactive children become partners in assessing their problems and behaviors, for they are asked to work with an adult to fill in dials that are missing from each meter. For each dial (numbered from 0 to 3), a rating of 0 indicates that the child feels there is a serious problem with that form of control, while 3 shows that he believes he is good at it. Although it might be perceived as gimmicky in some circles, sometimes that's what it takes to engage ADHDers. Working on the Concentration Cockpit could well help some children to consider, in novel fashion, their thinking and behavior, and to zero in on areas that need attention and improvement. Strengths are identified, which allow children to pick up on their good points, as well as "red flag" weaknesses. We don't have field test data on the Cockpit, but it is an interesting concept that one might adapt, study in a treatment setting, and build upon.

What metacognitive strategies, if any, should be used depends on many factors: the goals, the target behavior, the age of participants, and so on. Naturally, the cognitive level or development of the individual makes a big difference. One would not usually employ a complex metacognitive strategy with a very young child. There must be a mesh, where programming suggestions or exercises fit the stage of development of the ADHDer.

Indirect Intervention Strategies

Some very effective ways of dealing with overactive behavior are more subtle and indirect than the ones just discussed. In many instances, parents and teachers might do something to reshape the environment or the behavior of others to affect the overactive children. Of course, we're not attempting to draw hard and fast lines between direct and indirect strategies; sometimes the distinction between the two is fuzzy. However, we tend to view social skills training and verbal cues, for example, as direct because they're pretty up front, and nonverbal signals as more indirect and unobtrusive. While we're not setting firm guidelines or categories here, we'd like to spend some time on the following indirect approaches, which we view as more soft, gentle, and less invasive than the ones discussed so far:

Ask for Help!

Don't try to tackle ADHD alone: ask for help from relatives, colleagues, teachers, coaches, and significant others. Sometimes "outsiders" can see more than parents who are too close to the situation, and sometimes they may be able to offer ideas, encouragement, respite, and emotional support (important "assisters" indeed). Of course, you want reasoned and compassionate input, not dogma and diatribes. As Lincoln said, "He has the right to criticize who has the heart to help."

At school, teachers can sometimes get help from aides and volunteers. Peer tutoring can be useful as well, providing it is implemented carefully and supportively. Also, schools might consider recruiting and training cadres of mentors, some of who may be interested in working with overactive, distractible students. For hyper kids, a little one-to-one attention can go a long way, and a caring mentor can provide much needed emotional support. Mentoring has been found to be an effective technique for working with at-risk populations (Noller & Frey, 1995), and who could be more at risk than ADHDers? More comprehensive information about mentoring can be found in a variety of sources (Nash & Treffinger, 1993; Noller, 1982; Noller & Frey, 1994).

Nonverbal Cues

A classic study in the educational/social psychological literature is Rosenthal and Jacobson's (1968) *Pygmalion in the Classroom*. In this investigation, Rosenthal tested elementary students in the San Francisco school system and "identified" a number of "late bloomers" who, although they had shown no special abilities up to that time, were supposedly about to blossom at any moment. Teachers were told the testing had revealed that a select number of these students had hidden, latent potential that was about to burst forth and be fulfilled. But Rosenthal had done to the teachers what most social psychologists do in their experiments—he lied! The students in question really had shown nothing special during testing; they simply had been picked at random. Yet, when Rosenthal returned to the school the following year, he found that the IQs of these randomly selected "late bloomers" had in fact gone up. Essentially, then, self-fulfilling prophecy had been at work; the teachers got what they expected.

Why? How could such a thing happen? How could students' IQs possibly rise? The answer probably resides somewhere in the realm of nonverbal communication. Since teachers expected more of these specific students, they likely gave them more attention—an extra look, a glance, a pat on the back. As well, it was found that teachers gave these youngsters more time to formulate and articulate their thoughts rather than simply "cutting them off at the pass".

Later research indicates that the self-fulfilling prophecy effect is not as powerful as Rosenthal first suggested (cf. Goldenberg, 1992; McCluskey, 1986; McCormick & Pressley, 1997). He may well have been a victim of his own self-fulfilling expectations. Be that as it may, there is no denying that our attitudes do matter—we do often get what we expect, at least to a certain degree. This effect has even been demonstrated with animals. In one related study, graduate students in psychology were asked to teach rats how to run a maze (all psych. grad. students, in the course of their training, are asked to teach at least one rat to run a maze!). They were told that half the rats were genetically superior and specially bred to be "maze-bright". The other half were supposedly genetically inferior and "maze-dull". It was again a lie: there was no real difference between the groups of rats. Amazingly, however, the so-called "maze-bright" rats learned the task more quickly and efficiently than their "dull" counterparts. Somehow, the graduate students had communicated their expectations to the animals. Speculating a bit, what likely happened was that the "maze-bright" rats were picked up gently, given a pat, and—with a few soft words of encouragement—placed in the maze. In contrast, the "dull" rats were probably grabbed roughly, given a shake, and flung harshly into the same apparatus. Which animals are likely to learn better? In education, when it's kids we're dealing with, there's a need to pick them up gently and optimistically.

We want to stress again that the self-fulfilling prophecy effect, despite its intuitive appeal, has not been consistently supported in the literature (Goldenberg, 1992; McCormick & Pressley, 1997). That said, there is little doubt "low ability" students are treated differently from their supposedly more able counterparts. Perceived "low ability" children are more likely to be criticized by teachers, given terse answers, and seated at the back of the class. Further, when interacting with such labeled youngsters, educators have been shown to be less warm, less patient, and less likely to give them the benefit of the doubt (Brophy, 1985). Self-concepts of students rise when teachers believe in them and recognize their strengths (cf. Brophy, 1985; Brophy & Good, 1974; McCormick & Pressley, 1997).

Nonverbal signals can be amazingly subtle and have a tremendous impact on behavior (McCluskey, 2000b). They might also become cues for ADHD students, to help them curb rising impulses and stop bad behavior before it starts. And nonverbal messages can be "secret": a silent game played between the child and an adult. Raising an eyebrow, tapping a foot, or dropping a pencil might be part of the secret (which doesn't embarrass the child in public). A subtly raised index finger is a softer signal than a word or a yell. And, because of the novelty, ADHDers may pay more attention to nonverbals than to words.

To avoid embarrassing Amber, we developed a whole range of nonverbal signs, to which she still responds reasonably well. When all else fails, a good old-fashioned glare might be in order. We can get and maintain eye contact with Amber in social gatherings, and give her silent, but immediate feedback on her behavior (by a nod, grimace, wink, furrowed brow, smile, or frown).

Proxemics and personal space play a major role. Positioning the active child in the front of the classroom is usually a good strategy. That way, other children aren't in the line of sight (i.e., there's no one between the ADHDer and the board except the teacher), which minimizes distractions. As well, in the early stages of misbehavior—just when the wiggling is beginning—it's easy for the teacher to slide over and give the youngster a gentle tap on the hand or shoulder as a reminder. Simply walking into the child's personal space zone might be a "bad behavior nipper"—a signal to "whoa down" before things escalate.

Since nonverbals are so subtle, they don't always work with hyper kids (who often need concrete, "bang-them-over-the-head" stimuli). However, with Amber, they sometimes did, which made them valuable enough to keep in our repertoire.

Kinesthetic/Movement Approaches

We knew, almost from day one, that Amber simply had to move. It was as if there were five children in one body! The earlier description "driven by a motor" comes to mind. Until she was about seven or eight years of age, we were provided with a graphic illustration of this need every Christmas. Much to our amazement, Amber would start off Xmas morning "dare naked" (an example both of her uninhibited nature and b/d reversals), and then open gifts systematically, dressing as she went. We always made sure that undergarments were presented early. Being allowed to move in this fashion certainly made Christmas-time more festive and exciting for Amber. She was just as delighted to receive clothes as toys.

As mentioned previously, we could see Amber's need to move whenever she was asked to study. She didn't fare well with sit-still learning. Amber tried hard to concentrate, but would have to walk, hop, recite out loud, swing arms and legs, or sway back and forth (separately or all at once!). The routines were prodigious. We tried to get her to tone down the movement a bit, but it was impossible for her to concentrate without it.

Undoubtedly, Amber would learn more if she were able to focus in a quiet, structured setting. However, as a child, she just couldn't do that. Even today, she'll study in short bursts, take frequent breaks, move around a lot during recitation, and listen to music as she works. There's just no point fighting it. Some disjointed studying is better than none at all.

Howard Gardner (1983), in his pioneering work *Frames of Mind*, describes many types of "intelligences" or talents. Of the seven he first identified (others have cropped up of late), "bodily/kinesthetic" intelligence is particularly relevant for the ADHD child. For Amber, the "linguistic", "spatial", and "musical" dimensions are also important. Over the past few years, many curriculum or training packages have been based on Gardner's approach (check out any educational library), and some contain intriguing ideas for reaching students who typically don't do well in traditional academic settings.

While learning styles/modality theory has generated many divergent opinions and findings in the literature (cf. Eggen & Kauchak, 1994), Dunn and Dunn (1978) have insisted vehemently that movement is necessary for some children. Certainly, restructuring the environment to allow hyper kids to move, at least every now and again, seems to help. Despite the sit-still-and-be-quiet approach of law-and-order educators, restricting the movement of ADHDers typically doesn't work all that well. These students often end up being chastised repeatedly, disrupting the class on an ongoing basis, and getting "booted" for various intervals every couple of days.

Although it would be unfair and inappropriate to structure everything for the ADHDer, at times teachers can provide socially acceptable movement activities within the classroom. It is possible to intersperse such activities amid routine seat work. To illustrate, overactive (and other) youngsters might be assigned duties such as cleaning the chalkboard, sharpening pencils, or collecting papers. Even isometrics and some in-class play may be alternatives. Of course, one has to be cautious not to overdo it, but having diverse activities in the classroom can go a long way toward helping active students. Following the lead of Dunn and Dunn, some teachers try to match teaching to learning style (by allowing kinesthetic/tactile learners to use floppy beanbag chairs, sculpt with Play Doh, act out answers, and so on). Auditory learners might be permitted to listen to CD or cassette players (with headphones) while doing assignments. The debate still rages as to whether matching teaching to learning style is effective, and whether it is even possible to identify a learning style accurately in the first place. However, it seems safe to say that, since children learn differently, diversity is a plus in the classroom. Varying pedagogical style and activities (by changing the pace and using different media and modalities) allows teachers to reach and hold the attention of more students.

Some teachers rely heavily on a multi-modality (say it, show it, act it out) approach to lesson presentation, and they allow students to demonstrate their knowledge in different ways. During a science lesson on Leonardo da Vinci, for example, a teacher might first lecture, then show overheads, and finally use CD-ROM materials to make the topic come alive. Students might demonstrate understanding by writing down their ideas (perhaps using da Vinci's technique of "mirror writing"), drawing pictures, performing a skit, or even, singly or in groups, building their own version of one of his inventions (such as a model parachute, submarine, airplane, etc.).

Many educators believe strongly that varying activities in the classroom increases the chance that all children will have their needs met. Lesson plans have been developed to help teachers present material in different ways, using visual, auditory, and kinesthetic approaches (Barbe & Petreshene, 1981). All too often according to this perspective, when a child doesn't understand a lesson, we simply teach it again more slowly. Might it not be more valuable to teach it again differently?

Sister Mary Consilia (1978), in _The Non-Coping Child_, presented an excellent movement activity, called "Tents", which we still use today. Teaching concrete content through movement, "Tents" is employed at an early-years level to help children understand and build complex sentences. In this activity, six children in the class are given "tents" (pieces of soft cardboard, folded in half, which can stand on the desk or be held in front of them). One child gets the "Who?" tent, another the "Did What?" one, and so on through "Where?", "When?", "Why?", and "How?" Then the fun begins. The child with the "Who?" tent is called up: she'll come scurrying forward and be asked to make up the beginning of a sentence. Using Sister Consilia's illustration, she might stand, hold up her tent (to remind everyone she's a "Who?") and say "The three bears." The "Did What?" youngster can be called upon next: he'll stand beside the first child, and add to her bit—perhaps by saying, "went for a walk". "Where?" comes next ("in the park"), "How?" next ("quietly and without hurrying"), and so on. One can see the complex sentence building: "The three bears went for a walk in the park quietly and without hurrying ..." Through this exercise, children are taught that sentences can and should vary. To illustrate, if the teacher calls up the "How?" youngster first ("Quietly and without hurrying"), the structure of the sentence changes.

Creative educators can build on this and other activities. For example, by designing a movement lesson on punctuation, one child rolled into a ball might become a period, or two together (one "straight and stiff as a board" and the other "curled up") might be an exclamation point. Children could work alone or cooperatively to become commas, semi-colons, colons, or question marks, and gradually learn how to fit appropriately (perhaps between the "Tents" kids) into sentences.

In elementary school, one teacher and the principal developed a system where Amber became the official "note-runner". If a message had to be sent from the class to the office, Amber carried it. Even if no message was needed, when the teacher noticed Amber getting fidgety, she'd scribble meaningless words on a piece of paper and have Amber run the errand anyway. The principal could carry on without concern, knowing it was only Amber. And everybody was happy: Amber got a chance to move, notes were delivered when necessary, the teacher got a break from an active child every now and again, and there was a minimum of disruption in the class.

It is self-evident that visual and performing arts fit in here, and educational games can be used as well. Amber and other hyper kids often respond well to role plays, theater, music, and lip synching. A learning center approach can also be a boon for overactive youngsters; after completing one activity, they are allowed to move to the next. And there surely is a great deal of educational content in properly designed centers.

While movement and variety may suit ADHDers very well, it is still necessary to maintain control in the classroom. We're not recommending chaos, only flexibility for some part of the day. Undeniably, preparing movement, multi-modality, and center activities takes all kinds of planning—skilled, dedicated teachers are required.

Some active children excel at sports, where there's movement galore. Amber learned many lessons about planning, self-control, cooperation, and "staying cool" through basketball, football, and track and field.

There were times, however, where Amber's hyperactivity got the better of her even during sporting events. We're thinking of one football game in particular, where Amber was on the specialty team during kickoffs. Since she was the only girl, we were concerned. Some of those boys were giants (we're talking about three fellows on the offensive line with a combined weight of over a thousand pounds, and a combined height of the C.N. Tower). Dad refused to sign the waiver form (Amber hadn't yet turned 18), but Mom relented. So much for all that stuff about working together for consistent parenting! Every game was thrilling and anxiety-arousing.

Anyhow, because Amber's hair was tied and hidden under her helmet, the opposition didn't usually know at first that she was a female. Therefore, we urged our daughter to go about her business quietly, so as not to draw attention to herself. We didn't want her creating a disturbance or getting killed. Of course, that's not Amber's style—she lives to create disturbance. On the opening kick-off, she swerved around some blockers, circled from behind, gained ground rapidly, dove neatly, and tripped up the returner. Unbelievably, she had made a solo tackle. It would have been fine if she could have left it at that, but Amber—in her unrestrained exuberance— leapt up screaming: "Got the bastard!" We could have wished for a more unobtrusive approach.

High Interest Materials/Activities

To engage and hold the interest of "hyper" children, it is necessary to use motivating material and activities. In many cases, unusual, novel tasks are learned best because the kids are eager to focus on them. There is a danger, however, of overdoing it, and getting ADHDers too stimulated and excited. As always, one must strive for balance.

With Amber, we learned early to keep assignments short. Giving five minutes of work gained better results than overwhelming her with hour-long tasks. Lengthy assignments seemed impossible for her so, for many years, we opted to go the "short burst" route. Five minutes of something was better than an hour of nothing!

At school, or when helping Amber with work at home, it was essential to provide variety in lesson planning. For example, although she was abysmally weak when it came to word attack (phonics) in the middle years grades, there was no way we could hold her on task for an hour-long remedial session on this topic. Instead, whenever a "marathon session" was necessary, we talked to Amber for 10 minutes or so about her day, read to her for 15 minutes (to build in love of reading and the flow and rhythm of written language), tutored her directly on phonics for 10 minutes (using a cassette-workbook approach), and moved to "fun time" (where she'd read whatever she liked and could manage) for as long as she chose. We'd close with some short comprehension exercises (usually oral or multiple-choice) for a few minutes. Pacing of this type kept the kid focused to some extent.

Most overactive youngsters tend not to enjoy school work—they'd rather be playing or moving. They are rarely avid readers, but it's still often easier for some of them to focus on reading than on other academic subjects. Writing and math are typically "killers": both involve intense concentration, organization, and putting pencil to paper. As we've said, one sometimes sees a pattern where ADHDers, though well below grade level in all subjects, are better at reading than anything else. Of course, that's not always the case, particularly when learning disabilities are part of the syndrome.

In an effort to get Amber reading something, anything!, we started her off on high interest material—the Monster series. Those books were simple, and they had the stimulating feature of being accompanied by filmstrips and cassettes. An added bonus—Amber liked the romantic tone in *Monster Meets Lady Monster*. Although she couldn't read much of anything back then, Amber also liked watching the "movies" (the filmstrip-cassette that went along with each book). She gradually began to memorize words. While pure memorization may not be the ideal way to begin reading, it was a start. Once Amber had a working sight vocabulary, we could build from there. Very gradually, we moved on to more complex material.

We also used the old Sullivan corrective reading workbooks, in small doses, to try to develop specific skills. This structured approach can be painful for some students, but the paced, incremental, immediately-reinforcing framework did help Amber.

For the most part, though, we relied on high interest/low vocabulary material. By the time Amber had reached early junior high, the Pacesetters were popular in our schools. These high interest books contained mostly primary-level words, but the stories were intriguing enough to appeal even to adults. And while the vocabulary was carefully controlled, the novels weren't laid out in a "childish" way. These books provided a lot of excitement early, which is a plus for ADHD children, who don't want a book that sets the stage by describing, in grim detail, the uninspiring inner thoughts of a main character. They want to get down to business fast! When choosing books with Amber, we usually ended up with one in which something "big" happened on the first page.

In common with other series, each Pacesetters book came with an audiocassette. These were well done; the child heard the gunshots, the motorcycles revving up, or whatever. There was another neat little twist as well. Active children, being active children, tend to take the easy way out. They are interested and "hooked" by the sounds, but soon stop reading. In reluctant reader style, they listen to the audio and flip pages carelessly, without trying to read at all. Amber, for one, began her first Pacesetters book by doing far more listening than reading. At a singularly exciting point (at the close of the second chapter), however, the cassette abruptly ceased. Amber was extremely interested by this juncture, but, if she wanted to discover the ending, she had to read the last several chapters on her own. An insidious ploy. The format "hooked" her by working to an auditory strength before moving on to the weakness.

If truth be told, it's not only hyperactive children who have difficulty paying attention in our schools. Society has changed very much over the last few decades. The term "gentrification" has been used to describe our new reality, where "luxury" items once available only to the wealthy (or landed gentry) can now be obtained by all. Not that long ago, running water, fridges, stoves, and television were definite luxuries. In 1945, Gallup asked Americans if they knew what a television was; now most of us have one (or two, or three, or more) in our homes. Some time ago, we caught ourselves getting offended because the TV in our motel didn't have a remote. What deprivation! In a very real sense, the automobile revolutionized the American way of life (and teen-age dating patterns). More recently, there has been the advent of microwaves, VCRs, video games, and computers. Most of us today have access to these machines. As a result, children are now growing up in a very different world from that of their parents. Virtual reality has arrived.

In other words, like it or not, things have changed. A lot of kids spend an awful lot of time with their CDs, VCRs, DVDs, and video games. And whatever their faults, such devices undeniably entertain. It is not surprising to hear the comment from aging teachers, "The old things don't work any more; nobody listens." Of course they don't; the situation today is vastly different from what it was only a short time ago. We can no longer expect young children to sit meekly in rows while we dictate material to them. Their attention is likely to drift, and the problem will be exacerbated if they have a predisposition toward hyperactivity.

People talk about going "back to basics", but is that possible in light of the new realities, technologies, and expectations? Of course, one doesn't want to throw the baby out with the bath water; there are many excellent instructional methods of the past that should be retained by the educational system. But they must be adjusted in the new, changing context. There has been a massive paradigm shift and the world, as it must, continues to evolve. Rather than looking back in nostalgia, we should perhaps talk about moving "forward to basics". For better or for worse, the age of the one-room country schoolhouse is gone, and there is no going back.

Some special interest groups seem to think, however, if we could only go back to the one-room school house days, we'd find the cure-all for everything. But consider this analogy for a moment. Imagine you are going in for open-heart surgery, and decide—appropriately enough—to check out the surgeon. And imagine you were told this individual had made a great contribution to the discipline, and that he was at the top of his profession some 10 years ago. His skills have grown a trifle rusty over the last decade, but he really was wonderful in his time. You would be looking for a new doctor—somebody who is at the top of his profession now! In education, too, it is necessary to have teachers who build on the past by using new instructional approaches, equipment, and opportunities. Children of today need to be exposed to computers and new technology. The two of us tend to be conservative in our educational approach—we believe kids should learn to read, write, and do math. However, highly-skilled lecturers, if that is their only skill, might not do well in a high school of today. Kids now are used to being entertained by all sorts of stimulating gadgets. Why would they listen to somebody talk for an hour? To compete with other forces, we believe modern educators must teach basic skills in exciting, stimulating ways.

It is better to ask students what they are interested in rather than "tell" them. Whenever we went to a bookstore with Amber, she'd help choose her reading material. In that way, she was sure to end up with a book that she liked and could handle.

It's a good idea to observe ADHDers closely, noting well what tasks hold their attention. On one occasion in late junior high, "antsy" Amber surprised us. When she was confused about life in general, we asked her to write down her thoughts. And she did! She wrote a poem! Somehow, after all those years, Amber had finally developed the attention span to sit for long enough to produce something. She didn't like to write essays, but poetry captured her interest. The rhythm, the imagery, and the short length all suited her. As a little girl, she had loved listening to poetic songs, and she finally decided to try her hand at a poetic form of communication herself.

After that incident, Amber wrote poems regularly. We've decided to include a couple here, both produced just before she turned 16. A word of warning: the first poem is too weird to title. Amber makes it sound as if she is a sadistic, crazed dope fiend, which she isn't. But the poem gives some idea of how her mind works; try to keep up with her scattered thoughts!

Too Weird To Title

He stares like he's lost on the chair, gray and brown.
He reads contentedly alone on the moon.
Her heart must be broken, but she hides her pain.
Why look, don't run.
I can't see the man.
Maybe I should open my eyes.
Don't say love, fiery hair, hate in eyes!
She's not my type; get lost!
Cold chills, sweet taste, must be love!
Fun, face, sky, slurp, yummy!
Golden brown lengths.

Gribble, gribble, snort, gribble, blast;
Right now I am thinking that running is out and jumping is in.
Show the world your life, shun unhappiness!
Ha Ha kookle, blech, gribble, gribble, snort, dribble, blast.

Hee, Hee, Ha, Ha, laugh;
Tara bring it here! Turn around!
Greasy, slimy, yuck, dirty, scummy, gringy, yuck!

Hee haw! Hee haw Dog! Pandas are bears, not teddys, squishy!

Don't hug me, I hate you
Don't love me, I despise you
Just leave me to die!
I am at one with acid.
Lick it, taste it, sweet, sweet, sweet.
Your face is twisted, your face is deranged.
My God is acid, the drug not the rain!

Laughing, giggling, tingly feeling, spinning, crying, I'm high!
You wear your ring like a prize, but you have no morals;
don't let her tease you! Yup she's dirty.
Can I please gribble acid, pot, hash,
gotta love it, don't abuse it.

Am I crazy or insane?
God I hope I'm not crazy, just insane;
At least if I'm insane
I can still function in society,
Maybe a CEO of a company or something.

No, I suppose I'm neither;
I just see things for what they are; weird.
Playing safe just isn't safe anymore!

You can't handle life, I am death!
Deluxe! Stitch it up, don't dry your blood, have it rush!

The problem with some people is that they think they have to be
somebody everybody likes, or better than everybody. The flaw
in that theory is they're headed for a major crash. When reality
hits, people don't fail; they become real!

Yabba Dabba Doo!

The second effort is more sedate. Not professional by any means, but
interesting. And certainly both poems indicate that, in contrast to the dire
predictions, Amber is far from functionally illiterate.

Time

The snowy swings and the blue teeter-totter have been
abandoned; for tomorrow the sun may shine or it may not.

Soon the snow melts away, revealing yet another family park
that was once filled with happy children and gentle laughter.

Swings sway in the breeze; leaves soon cover one end of the
teeter-totter.

Where are the children who once occupied this quiet park?
Where are the voices that filled the air with life?

> Time is the only answer.
> People grow.
> Children become human.

As indicated earlier, one other interest that has had a major impact on our daughter's life was music. Dad and Mom were old-folkie types, and—due to their influence—Amber has become a prisoner of the '60s. When she was in the primary grades, one album in particular captured her fancy. Donovan's *For the Little Ones* is aptly titled: Amber would clean her room, do her homework, and fall asleep to strains of *The Mandolin Man and His Secret*, *The Enchanted Gypsy*, *The Lullaby of Spring*, and all the other lyrical songs on that record. An ADHD kid who couldn't read, Amber was still able to learn about the beauty of language, about poetry, and about perspectives on life from this wonderful album. When she was "rangy", it soothed her. It still does.

The point is that it's easier to work with ADHDers on something they're interested in than on something they loathe and despise. If Amber liked a book, we got it (one of the cardinal rules in our home is "Never say no to a book!"). If she enjoyed a sport, we supported it. And if she wanted to write poems, we read 'em.

Kind Firmness

As paradoxical as it sounds, we believe that the technique of "kind firmness" is one of the best ways to cope with overactivity. Years ago, we ran across an excellent quotation in *Reader's Digest* (the ultimate source of all knowledge). We can't recall exactly, but it went something like this: "Good discipline is like holding a wet bar of soap: if your grasp is too loose, it falls from your hand, but if you squeeze too tightly, it also slips away." That's the challenge with ADHDers—one has to walk a tightrope between keeping them in line and letting them have a life.

In any approach to discipline, it's important to respect the pace of the child. The first author found it easy to take when seven-year-old Amber said to him, "Dad, when I grow up, I want to marry you." That sort of statement is okay, for it reflects the young child's level of development. It wasn't quite so happy an occasion for Dad when capricious 16-year-old Amber demanded he pull the car "way out of sight" before dropping her off for school. She didn't want any of her friends to see that "My father is an old, long-haired hippie." No, not so palatable, but still okay. The statement reflects a different stage of development. We've mentioned other examples where we've respected Amber's pace (by letting her play with dolls that she might have been considered "too old for", and not rushing her into getting her driver's license).

One flash of parenting insight came to us when taking Amber to the Manitoba Museum of Man and Nature. Actually, we were looking for an excuse to leave a hectic family reunion, so we began to pack up Amber and Chris, aged seven and eight at the time, for an exciting museum visit. We were stunned to find that many of the relatives, knowing Amber as they did, had strong feelings about the matter. Aunts and uncles, cousins, and others echoed the same warning: "You can take Christopher, but you can't take Amber!" When we queried "Why?", the reaction was: "Goodness, it's a beautiful building. There'll be nothing left! She'll destroy it all!"

After reflecting on the situation, we decided we were damn well going to take Amber. She was undeniably difficult, but it seemed to us that a seven-year-old, no matter what her problems, shouldn't be totally out of control in a public place. We recommend never getting into a power struggle with a child but, on this occasion, we decided that if there had to be a clash of wills, we were going to win. Physically, at least, we knew there would be no difficulty—we were bigger.

Armed with this size advantage, we toddled off to the museum, both kids in tow. Our plan was simple. While Mom watched over Chris, Dad would take Amber by the hand and, come hell or high water, not let go. The moment we passed through the entrance, Amber tried to take off in her usual rambunctious fashion. However, Dad hung on. Amber made a second attempt, and Dad—gently, but firmly—kept a grip on her hand. Eventually she realized that she was going to pull her arm out of the socket before Dad would let go. Although Amber was physically restrained, it wasn't done negatively. We thoroughly enjoyed walking along together, reliving history, and moving from exhibit to exhibit.

After a spell, Amber said: "Daddy, if you let me go look at the wolf, I'll come right back." After a quick parental consultation, we did let her go—and she returned as promised. Little Amber had gotten the idea. While we don't mean to imply that this automatically fixed everything, it was a beginning.

Along the same lines, we have also made liberal use of Dreikurs' theory of logical consequences (Dreikurs & Grey, 1968). With this framework, you let the consequence fit the crime—the outcomes for children are tied directly to their behavior. Two examples spring to mind.

In the first, we were having difficulty getting Amber ready in the morning in time for her school bus (perhaps some readers can relate to this dilemma). Although we always woke her up in plenty of time, she got into so many things throughout the morning that she was invariably late. Indeed, we usually found ourselves with an awful feeling in the pits of our stomachs—each day it was a battle trying to get this child ready for the bus. When she was in grade 3, we spent half of the year—well into January—living in anxiety and fighting the bus fight.

Eventually we realized that what we had here was a question of "problem ownership". We were taking full responsibility for getting Amber ready, without putting any of the onus on her. There were no consequences for noncompliance. Determined to right matters, we made an adjustment.

In a frank family discussion, we pointed out that henceforth we expected Amber to be ready in time for the bus, period! It was her responsibility, and she would be given only a couple more warnings at most (we usually try to give two warnings). It was easy to establish the consequence in this instance: what should happen if you miss the school bus? ... You walk! It's critical that the consequence is logical. It doesn't do to tell a child, "If you don't clean your room, I'll break your legs!" She knows that's not going to happen. To put it another way, one can't threaten, one must act. And if one is to act, the consequence must be reasonable.

We were comfortable with the situation in question. It was a fair distance to the school, about a mile from our place, but the walk was definitely doable. And, of course, Amber—pushing things to the limit—missed twice more. We drove her each time, uttering warnings all the way. Then, inevitably, she was late yet again.

We responded. As it happened, on the day of the third miss, the weather was decidedly unpleasant. Although not precisely a blizzard, it was windy, icy, and cold. And there were safety issues to consider, for the walk to school included a stretch along the highway. Exercising parental responsibility all the while, we followed through by bundling Amber up and having her make the trek (as we drove slowly alongside her the entire way!). She rarely missed the bus thereafter.

The second example took place just a short time later, when we went as a family to a Gondola Pizza restaurant somewhere on Pembina Highway. We don't remember the exact location, but it doesn't matter—we can never go back! Quite simply, the kids were terrible: they were noisy, disruptive, and rude. Amber, in particular, got out of hand. She yelled, made faces, jumped about, and needlessly spilled her drink. Both kids ignored our first two warnings, so we followed through once more. What is the logical consequence if you can't behave in a restaurant? You don't eat!

We waited until the pizza was brought to the table, so that both Amber and Chris could look at it, smell it, and almost taste it. However, we then plunked our money down, got up, and—in a grandiose gesture— left the pizza sitting there. Dad was mad as blazes, but remembering the rule never to punish in unrestrained anger, said calmly: "Too bad you couldn't behave; we'll have to try again another day." When we got home the children were sent up to bed without supper, and Mom and Dad hit the refrigerator.

It may be inadvisable to use it, but food sure is a powerful reinforcer. The next morning, both kids came down in rather contrite fashion. But wouldn't you know it, they started acting up again at the breakfast table. This time it was Mom who said, "Oh, are we going to have to try again at lunch?" There was instant silence and good behavior from that point on. The kids knew we were capable of following through, and food deprivation was in our arsenal. Ever since, we've been able to take them to any restaurant, no matter how elegant, and expect and get excellent behavior.

In fairness to Amber, we relaxed the rules considerably at home, where she was usually allowed to flop, move, and enjoy informal mealtimes. However, we didn't think it was too much to ask that she behave, for an hour or so, on special occasions and outings. We saw no reason to be embarrassed in public, even by an ADHD child. Our goal was always to be as positive as possible, but also to have expectations.

In our approach to kind firmness, we sometimes made use of the concept "choice within limits" (Ginott, 1969). Let us illustrate. One of our acquaintances, tremendously pleased with his approach, once announced that he was an "enlightened" parent who allowed his four-year-old daughter to choose all of her own clothing. The result was often quite ludicrous: she decked herself out in the strangest of outfits. To our minds, this was negligence, not enlightenment. Following Ginott's advice, what we did when Amber was younger was say: "Here are three dresses that are acceptable to us; you can pick one." In going about things in this manner, we encouraged her gradually to become more independent, and still provided parental guidance, direction, and supervision. In time, we let her make more and more choices on her own.

When the time was right, we also used "reflective listening" (Dinkmeyer & McKay, 1976), where we listened hard, responded empathically, and encouraged sharing. Figuratively speaking, the goal is to hold up a mirror in front of children, reflect back their feelings, and show that you understand.

With reflective listening, it's important to keep communication open. For example, when Amber came home in tears, sobbing "Billy and the other kids won't play with me", it would have been easy to answer with "Well, that's too bad, but that's the way things go," or "That's part of life; don't worry about it." Although those sorts of responses may be intended kindly, they often close the communication. A more open response, one that reflects the feelings expressed and encourages more interaction, would be "You're feeling hurt and left out." Hearing that, Amber would know we understood and be encouraged to go on.

We don't use the reflective listening approach a great deal. When overdone, it makes us feel artificial, as if we're acting. We believe parents have the right to be angry and to communicate their anger to their children. Wild, unrestrained hostility is obviously to be avoided, but honest displeasure can be okay. And sometimes we expect the kids to "Sit down and listen." We have neither the time nor the inclination to attempt to negotiate or be sensitive about every little thing. Still, there are instances when listening reflectively can truly help you tune in. During bedtime discussions in particular, we liked to use the approach. It forced us to focus on what the kids were saying, and certainly it got them to talk, share their feelings, and go to bed happily.

At a presentation a couple of years back, Amber was asked by some teachers what they could do to make the lot of ADHDers easier. Her empowering response: "Just be nice." Sometimes, obsessed with strategies, programs, organization, and rules, we underestimate the "therapeutic power of kindness", but it is profound (Long, 1997).

Flexible Structure

Again paradoxically, we relied heavily on flexible structure in our interactions with Amber. As many educators have noted before us, attention deficit children need structure and specific routines. Directions should be kept short and simple (and it's not a bad idea to have youngsters repeat instructions to make sure they have grasped them). Tasks should be simplified, such that complex or abstract activities are broken down into component parts. Short one- or two-step directions are preferable. In school, after explaining instructions to the class as a whole, it is usually wise to go back and repeat key points to the active, distractible child on a one-to-one basis.

Rules are essential, but we didn't want Amber to be a prisoner of structure. Although we couldn't let her run wild, we wished her to be happy. After all, childhood should be fun. At home, we only used tight structure and extreme control when it came to issues of safety and respect. Important rules were enforced in a firm way; less critical ones were "loosey-goosey".

Going back to our earlier meal examples, we expected Amber to be well-behaved when we were in public. Even ADHD children can learn that while they might get away with certain behavior in some situations, it is unacceptable in others. We realized Amber couldn't be Little Miss Manners all the time. Meals at home really were informal. If we ate at the table, we encouraged discussion, joking, and a very happy tone. Much of the time, the kids ate on the floor, in their rooms, or in front of the television. When we rented movies, we tried to make a production of it, complete with buttered popcorn. Often we'd all "camp" and fall asleep in the living room. The rules could be bent or suspended at such times. On other occasions, though, we meant business, we demanded more, and we expected Amber to understand and comply.

We took a hard line with vulgar language, feeling that respectful speech is part of respectful behavior. Again, kids can understand that certain language they might get away with in the locker room or on the playground is inappropriate in the classroom. And certainly, we didn't want to hear many four-letter words around our place. We once caught Amber using the dreaded "F word" with kids in the yard. She pointed out, perhaps quite rightly, that we shouldn't have gotten so upset—after all, "It's just a word." But it's not a word we wanted to hear coming out of her mouth on our property. Again, we weren't going to order Amber never to use bad language; most people seem to, and one has to fit in. However, we did expect her to use judgment; certain actions are less heinous in some situations than in others. We asked that she note the circumstances and respond accordingly.

In school, we hope for reasonable structure, but not a prison camp. The once-popular open area classrooms are obviously not ideal for overactive youngsters—there's simply too much stimulation. However, kids-in-rows-all-day-every-day isn't ideal either—it can be just too confining. Amber had trouble keeping her body still, and even when she did, her mind wandered. Without some respite, her life in regimented classrooms would be a living hell. Again, the goal must be to achieve a happy medium.

As the first author has noted in an article entitled *Lines in the Sand* (McCluskey, 2000a), some educators seem fixated on rules, regulations, and treating everyone the same. But that's not the way it works in real life, where most everyone recognizes that people and abilities differ: we do not expect a 300-pound offensive lineman to dash 50 yards down field to receive a pass in a football game; we do not require all artists to paint portraits; and we do not want the Dixie Chicks to sound like Marilyn Manson. Why, then, is it such a stretch to acknowledge and respond to individual differences in some classrooms?

Certain law-and-order educators pride themselves in taking a zero tolerance approach in their schools. Naturally, we can't let anarchy prevail—there must be rules and order in any institution. Curwin (1999) has asked, however: "Would we want our partner in life to have zero tolerance? Would we want to teach our own children to have zero tolerance?" An inflexible policy, which fails to take into account the circumstances and overall social context, can limit options, box us in, and interfere with the search for creative alternatives. Yes, there must be consequences, but it's nice to have some wiggle room as well.

Part of the art of working with hyperactive students is being sensitive and looking for "teachable moments". For much of the day, hyper youngsters will not be able to focus. At certain times, though, something may grab their attention, and they're suddenly in the mood to concentrate and learn. Teachers must be flexible enough to strike while the iron is hot. Adhering rigidly to structured lesson plans won't do the trick; good teachers adapt and seize opportunities when they present themselves.

Other modifications are possible and not that onerous. Why not modify tests for ADHDers, at least some of the time? Long answer, essay-type exams are deadly for them. Every now and again, let active kids take oral tests to demonstrate what they know. It can be surprising to hear some of the knowledge they have acquired. Multiple-choice type tests also work better for some youngsters, who can attack these questions in smaller chunks.

We think it is reasonable and necessary, both at home and at school, to intervene to help support social relationships for hyperactive children. We've discussed how, all too often, hyper kids lack friends. They want them, but they don't know how to get them or keep them. Their behavior frequently turns people off. At home, we knew Amber had difficulty with relationships, so we'd seek out empathic peers who were willing to "put up with her". Some kids are understanding enough that, if you explain the situation to them, they will bend over backward to help another child in distress. As Amber got a little older, we actually stooped to "buying" popularity for her. We were fortunate enough to have the means to put in a swimming pool, which ensured that she would have frequent visitors and "friends". It was a pain to supervise some of the youngsters, but it helped Amber maintain relationships. It also kept her close at hand, where we could keep an eye on her.

At home, we've also found other partial substitutes for friends—most notably pets. Amber loves animals (recall the infamous kissing dog incident): through her childhood and adolescence, she had six cats (Frisky, Pete, Repete, Quesadilla, Elmo, and Sprite) and two wonderful dogs (Colby and Dulcinea, whose ashes now rest on her mantel). On her 8th birthday, she got Dulcinea, the little cross-terrier who remained her faithful companion for 17 years.

Colby, a gigantic Samoyed who died long ago, would join forces with Dulcinea to protect his little mistress. Honestly, we couldn't raise our voices or lay a hand on the kid in anger if the dogs were anywhere in the vicinity. If we approached Amber with evil intent, Colby—usually a laid-back type of animal—would push us away. And Dulcinea, generally extremely calm, would jump between, bare her teeth, and growl menacingly. Amber was not to be threatened in any way.

Our daughter had a tendency to save and adopt any animal that was in danger. We've had an assortment of injured birds, rabbits, and squirrels foisted on us for various intervals, and Elmo (who was hyper himself) and Sprite took up permanent residence after she rescued them. Her animals meant a great deal to Amber. At times when she didn't have other friends, she had them. Of course, there is a price to be paid. The wear and tear on curtains and furniture has been incredible. Despite such inconveniences, however, we'd seriously recommend that parents of ADHDers with relationship problems consider getting a pet to help see their children through the difficult, lonely times. If you make the kids partly responsible for the care and feeding of their animals, they can also learn valuable lessons about responsibility.

At school, too, we consider it totally legitimate to try to support friendships for the ADHDers. Some teachers have told us that they don't feel it's part of their job to find friends for overactive students; we disagree. Helping hyper kids develop friendship skills is one of the most important things anybody could do for them. If overactive students are to improve their behavior, they must have some sort of positive interaction with peers. Counselors usually have access to interesting kits and materials designed to help in relationship building and interpersonal communication. Several books also bear on this issue (Forman, 1993; Stephens, 1992).

We advise teachers who have an active child in their class to look first at the structure of the room. To illustrate, let's assume we have an energetic, committed teacher on the scene. Such enthusiastic educators often go to great lengths to make their rooms stimulating. Indeed, one can't take a step without being hit on the head by a mobile. Books abound (a good idea), posters cover the walls, samples of students' work are plastered all over the bulletin board and elsewhere, and often an ant colony or hamster cage is on display. If there is the luxury of windows, there is usually bright sunlight pouring in on this happy scene, and often decorations adorning the panes. Most of these things are extremely positive, and we wouldn't quarrel with using this approach for most children. If teachers are happy in their classrooms and doing what they believe in, things are likely to work. Certainly, we've seen many teachers of this type who make learning come alive.

On the downside, though, consider for a moment the plight of an overactive youngster in such a setting. Due to attentional problems, such a child is apt to be overwhelmed, confused, and driven to distraction.

Therefore, without changing their entire style or modus operandi, we recommend that teachers faced with such students make subtle adjustments (for the year the ADHDer is in the class). For example, it may be wise to move the active child away from the window—gazing out might simply be too distracting. At home, we find that Amber can't get anything done near a window. If she's to have any hope at all of attending to task, she has to put her study desk against the wall. Getting back to the class situation, it also isn't a bad idea to place such a student in the front row, where a large measure of proximity control can be exercised. As we've said, the teacher can walk by and give a little tap on the shoulder or other nonverbal signal if the child is beginning to get out of hand. It might also be worthwhile to draw the foremost blind and move the posters further back in the room, so that the hyperactive child (who ideally should be looking forward) won't be distracted. And finally, the hamsters or ants might be moved to the rear corner, and perhaps hidden behind a divider. As a reward, youngsters can go to the back and observe or play with these creatures, but they shouldn't be focusing on them during lesson time. Simple changes of this type may reduce extraneous, competing stimuli and help the ADHDer pay more attention to academic work.

Although they didn't necessarily have ADHD in mind, some educators have recommended restructuring entire schools (Renzulli, 1994; Treffinger, 1998). At the secondary level, it is possible—by going to the Copernican "quarter system"—to restructure the use of time, alter the school day and schedule, reduce classroom size, and focus on individualized learning. It is becoming popular in some high schools to teach one subject in the morning and one subject in the afternoon—that's it. Four times a year, students deal with two subjects per day. Although there are always pluses and minuses, think of the advantages for hyperactive students. They can interact and bond with a couple of staff members at a time, rather than be overwhelmed by six or seven. They know where they're supposed to be at all times, and don't have the confusion of having to switch constantly from classroom to classroom. And they can keep themselves organized: they don't have to figure out what day of the cycle it is or what books they should have with them.[†]

---

† Detailed information about this approach is presented elsewhere (Carroll, 1989).

Common Mistakes

How well do parents and teachers respond to overactive children? Sometimes not very well at all! It's easy to become frustrated, angry, hostile, and abrupt. Valett (1974), to help educators assess how well they're meeting the needs of their hyperactive students, developed a teacher self-rating form. Rather than simply looking at the child's actions, instruments of this type encourage adults to consider their own behavior as well. Do we act calm in the presence of children, or anxious? Do we model reason, or irrationality? Do we behave consistently, or hysterically, in our interactions with students and colleagues?

Several educators have identified some mistakes and errors of judgment that we, as adults, commonly make in dealing with ADHD children. In our opinion, if we can identify our own shortcomings, we're halfway there in terms of working with difficult students. Once we know the problem, it's possible to adjust and improve. Therefore, borrowing, adapting, and extending from the work of DeBruyn and Larson (1984) and others, we'd also like to delineate and discuss some of these typical mistakes. They are

(1) Assuming that ADHD children can easily control their behavior. They can't; it's part of who they are. Of course, one goal is to gradually help ADHDers gain more control, but we can't expect that to happen overnight.

(2) Administering unfair and overly harsh punishment. In an effort to "correct" behavior, some parents and teachers are just too hard on overactive youngsters. Soften the "spare the rod, spoil the child" dictum for these kids, or prepare for disaster. Discipline is, of course, essential, but it must be flexible and supportive as well as firm.

(3) Humiliating hyperactive children, intentionally or otherwise. Often parents and teachers belittle ADHDers in front of their friends or classmates. Even nonverbally, it's possible to create embarrassment (by grimacing at their efforts, always moving their desks out into the hall, etc.). One must help ADHDers maintain their self-concept. "Put-downs" are destructive. As others have said, one of the great challenges is to treat difficult, sometimes disrespectful kids respectfully.

(4) Assuming hyper kids are always to blame. Overactive children often get a "bad rep", to the point where adults, virtually automatically, blame everything on them. This form of prejudice is inappropriate. In Amber's case, although she was frequently guilty, there were many instances when it was a "bum rap". Frequently, she was held accountable for incidents at home and at school that she'd had nothing to do with. Her brother and classmates found it ridiculously easy to set her up, and they did. When we took the time to listen reflectively, we were surprised to find how often she was innocent.

(5) Behaving inconsistently. In working with overactive youngsters, some of us need to loosen up, while others have to tighten up. There is a need to strike a consistent balance, so expectations are clear.

(6) Assigning impossible tasks. ADHDers have trouble with "chain commands", lengthy assignments, and concentrating for long periods of time. Don't overwhelm them with things they can't possibly manage. Build slowly upon little successes and gradually increase the difficulty level of activities.

(7) Being inflexible. To some people, the rules or standards seem to mean more than common sense and basic humanity. Children are more important than rules or marks; sometimes it's necessary to adjust and adapt to meet the special needs of individual students. To think that the home or school must be the same for everyone is naive and narrow. ADHDers can't be allowed to "run the ship", but they do require flexibility. Sometimes social-emotional needs should take precedence over academic ones. Some of the elementary teachers who fared best with Amber were the ones who "loved her up". Even in the secondary grades, rules should be bent every now and again!

(8) Failing to go that extra mile for the child. Some parents and teachers feel it's unnecessary or improper to do "little extras" for ADHD children. Others can't seem to get up enough energy to go above and beyond the call of duty. Special gestures and kindness can go a long way. It's worth the time and effort. And if you have to deal with an ADHDer, eat well, keep fit, and get your rest—a high energy level is a requirement.

(9) Avoiding asking for help. With ADHDers, two or more well-intentioned heads can be better than one. Form partnerships, collaborate, and call on others.

(10) Losing your sense of humor. If one can maintain perspective, it's possible to enjoy (preferably vicariously) all the things that happen when working with ADHD children. Appreciate and savor the improbable situations that arise. If you lose your sense of humor along the way, you're doomed—you're going to need it!

Chapter 5

A MODEL FOR OUR HOME

By now, we hope it's clear that we've worked as a family to guide Amber in her journey through hyperactivity. To help all of us along the way, we adopted our own philosophy, or approach, or model. Call it what you will, it was important enough to us that we've given it a name, and used it as something to live by.

Using SMARTS to Parent ADHD Children

To cope with Amber, we had to put SMARTS into our parenting. Our acronym stands for Special Moments, Acceptance, Respite, Time, and Sharing. These strategies are good for all kids, but they were especially helpful in keeping us on track with our hyperactive daughter.[††] We'll spend the rest of this chapter addressing each of the SMARTS components:

Special Moments

Hyperactive kids need variety and excitement or they become bored. However, they're not the only ones who require fun, stimulation, and a change of pace; we all do. Of course, we're talking about reasonable levels of stimulation, not holding up gas stations.

In our family, we've always attempted to build in special moments through travel; taking a few trips a year can be highly pleasurable.

[††] A few years after first writing about SMARTS (McCluskey & McCluskey, 1996), we discovered that Nylund (2000), coincidentally, had proposed a more recent SMART model of his own. Through that framework, part of his narrative therapy approach, he focused on Separating the problem from the child (by carefully altering language to reduce blaming and externalize the ADHD), Mapping the impact of the condition on the youngster and family (to give the child some awareness and control over the situation), Attending to exceptions to the ADHD story (by emphasizing positive times when the child has coped successfully), Reclaiming the special talents of the ADHDer (by highlighting the strengths), and Telling the new story (thereby celebrating successes with a significant audience and giving the child's tarnished reputation a make-over). An interesting formulation, but vastly different from ours.

Besides, travel is a learning experience. Amber knows how to behave at social gatherings in various countries, she understands different cultural points of view, and she seeks out and treasures friends from other places. Through travel, she has been able to see and learn much that she never could have acquired in school. Travel means movement, and that's how Amber learns best. Things she may not have been able to understand in books she has experienced and absorbed firsthand.

On our travels, we made young Amber the cartographer: she'd gradually learn where she was from, where she had been, and where she was going. And the map skills certainly helped her with directionality. Amber also found acceptance in far-off places: with her exuberant personality, she fit in well in some other cultures. Amber was seen as highly emotional and volatile here, but as delightful in Mexico. On all the trips, she had many special moments—not only with us, but with newfound friends. Her circle of significant others grew dramatically (which was important for a child with few friends at home).

Of particular significance to us is Disney World. It was our first trip; the place where we truly bonded and came together as a family. We can still picture little Amber, crying as we left on the ferry at vacation's end. She felt that "We'll never be back to such a nice place." When we saw what the trip had meant to her and how she had blossomed during it, we vowed to return. And we have, repeatedly. The Disney obsession and visits never get boring for her, so they can never be boring for us.

Of course, we can already anticipate the criticism: "Well, that's fine for you—you have the means to travel." That's true in part, but it's also true that it can be a matter of establishing priorities. We don't spend a whole lot on drinking, gambling, or wild living on the home front, so we can put something away for our hard-earned special moments. Noting how "reaffirming" travel is for Amber, we've gone into debt to make sure she got her holiday trips. It's amazing where you can go if you make the effort.

However, special moments don't have to be particularly exotic, just enjoyable. Most parents can at least drive with their kids to another city, to the countryside, or to visit relatives. In a quest for something different, we were once able—through careful planning—to take the kids to four movies in one day. Silly, but memorable (and special nonetheless).

It's a rare community that doesn't have opportunities for walking, sightseeing, camping, or whatever. We have worked with some single parents, in particular, who really didn't have extra cash on hand to do much with their kids; they were living from hand to mouth. Still, they managed to build in variety and excitement by, once a week, taking the youngsters to McDonald's. All kids seem to love McDonald's.

Far afield or in the home, special moments change the pace, give children something to look forward to, and leave them with indelible memories to cherish. Because ADHDers can encounter so many frustrations, failures, and disappointments, it's absolutely necessary to build in these special, positive occasions in their young lives.

Acceptance

Keeping in mind Maslow's (1970) Hierarchy of Needs, not much can happen for youngsters until they feel safe and secure in their environment. Acceptance is critical. In client-centered terms, we're speaking of "unconditional positive regard" (Rogers, 1951).

As we so often remark, some teachers have been frustrated with us because they feel we haven't been tough enough on Amber at home. However, in our opinion, Amber faced an abundance of discipline everywhere else. Although we set consistent, realistic guidelines, we did so following our principle of "kind firmness". Our little girl needed a haven; a bastion where she was cared for and safe. Adherents of the "tough love" approach might not approve, but we always told Amber that "Home is home". She'd receive support there no matter what. We might disapprove of her behavior, set some rather firm guidelines, and mete out consequences, but we would never, no matter what the provocation, abandon her or ask her to leave home.

Of course, once Amber was in senior high, there were dangers—boys and drugs to name two. We had faith in Amber's standards, and never thought she'd be "loose" or into drugs. Still, at the time, her judgment wasn't consistent, and sex, drugs, and rock and roll can be enticing. Many parents who don't expect it suddenly find that their daughter is pregnant or abusing drugs. If either had happened to Amber, home would still have been home. That was unconditional. In the meantime, we watched her like hawks to make sure those things didn't happen, and she went about her business secure in the knowledge that she was accepted somewhere.

Respite

In providing for ADHD children, one must strike an ever-elusive balance. We didn't want to get too absorbed in Amber, for that wouldn't be healthy for her or anybody else. The world could not revolve solely around her. Chris required equal time, and we needed some as well. Consequently, we made sure to fit in perks for ourselves—some together-without-the-kids moments. While we gave both kids plenty of attention, they didn't get it all. Parents must not smother their children; kids need their space and an opportunity to become independent.

Early during Amber's high school years, Dad and Mom took a brief trip to Grand Cayman. We needed a respite! We found, however, that it was difficult to get Amber out of our thoughts. While on tour at a Cayman conservation farm, we stopped to observe the baby turtles in a tank—there were literally thousands of them. Immediately, we both espied one frantic little turtle. The creature in question was turning, spinning, bumping, bouncing off the walls, and disrupting the entire tank. Simultaneously, we looked at one another and muttered, "Amber!" It was then we realized, even in mid-respite, how much we missed her.

Time

Many parents worry about sibling rivalry. Although some rivalry among sibs is natural, it can be minimized by making sure that there's plenty of time to go around. If children each receive the attention they need, they're not likely to be at each other's throats. It's when it becomes a case of "scarce supplies", where time is severely restricted, that battles are likely to ensue.

Because both of us were always terribly busy with our work, we had to make some adjustments to ensure that we gave the kids the time they needed. ADHDers like Amber can't pay attention, so they require much more of it. By the same token, their sibs shouldn't be neglected. Chris needed his "piece of the action" too.

As Kennedy, Terdal, and Fusetti (1993, p. 103) note, brothers and sisters of ADHDers rarely have an easy time of it: they are "normal children who do not lead normal lives ... almost always they feel their life is unfair". When we think about the demands hyperactive kids place on the parents, we're not surprised. Kennedy, Terdal, and Fusetti also observe that siblings of hyperactive children live with many pressures and challenges. They may end up hiding toys and possessions that otherwise would be appropriated, damaged, or lost; they may be faced with an ADHD intruder who will, as a matter of course, "butt in" on their special moments with parents; and they may consistently be given "the short end of the stick" in terms of time, space, and attention. Resentment often rears its ugly head because rules and expectations are not the same for each child. Embarrassment typically surfaces as well, for siblings of ADHDers are often hesitant to invite friends over. To further compound the problems, there may be no one to turn to for comfort. Besieged parents do tend to get wrapped up in the life of the "problem child", and usually there are no peers who can relate to the distress. As a result, siblings may view themselves, with some justification, as hard done by. Sadly, their pain is largely invisible to others, and they frequently suffer in silence.

We feel truly blessed that Chris, a calm, independent sort, was a wonderful brother to Amber. Aside from that brief time in junior high, when—dismayed by her behavior—he disowned his sister, Chris was always Amber's staunchest supporter. Indeed, he emerged as her protector and watchdog. Chris's self-sufficient style helped, as did the fact he was a superior athlete who received plenty of accolades for football and basketball. We got to most of his games, and sports provided a mechanism for giving him his own place in the sun.

We know Chris felt it, however. We wanted and always intended to give him every bit as much attention as Amber got, but it wasn't easy (and we probably never did manage things equitably). With the needs of our daughter sucking us dry, our son undoubtedly had his share of crosses to bear. Chris's point of view can be found in much more detail in another publication (McCluskey, McCluskey, McCluskey, & McCluskey, in press).

Amber owes Chris a great debt, and she knows it. Her brother became her role model, and she tried her best to emulate him in school, on the football field and basketball court, and in selecting a career. Chris, for his part, gained from supporting and coping with Amber over the years. He learned lessons about empathy, kind firmness, and flexible structure that helped him grow into a strong teacher and coach, one comfortable working with at-risk young people. Today he is well-equipped to deal compassionately, yet firmly, with recalcitrant students.

When the kids were quite young, we caught ourselves focusing too much on our careers and not enough on our family. It's painfully easy to become overdedicated to a job and underdedicated to the things that matter more. Educators, in particular, often give so much to others that they neglect their own. After working with children all day, they come home and don't want to see another child. Yet, their own kids await. We didn't want to rationalize or use the we-spend-"quality-time"-with-the-kids line as an excuse for not really spending "enough time" with them.

As a result, we curtailed or cut back other activities. Dad loves "playing the links", but there was a decade of golf taken out of his life. There's more time for that now. Mom loves arts and crafts, but she held back until the kids were older. We've had opportunities to join various groups or service clubs, but always opted not to. Any spare time we had went to our kids. We don't suggest giving up all outside pursuits, but when time is tight one's family should come first. If there's a hyper child in the mix, it's going to take plenty of time to put and keep your house in order.

Good parents, by definition, advocate and support their children when necessary. But some people spend too much time advocating and lobbying for their children, and not enough time with them (one reason there is no "advocacy" section in this book).

Most Sunday mornings, we went for breakfast with the kids. When we arrived home, we often tacked on impromptu events: a family game of football in the yard, basketball in the driveway, a car ride, a visit to grandparents, or, of all things, collecting beer bottles from the ditches (Amber, motivated by movement, and Chris, motivated by money, both loved that).

Whenever our youngsters were involved in sports, we tried to encourage them by watching their teams (it was rare for us to miss a football or basketball game) or playing with them on our own. On family trips, we devoted ourselves to the kids. And although neither of us enjoyed it quite as much, we helped with school when called upon (or when periods of "forced learning" were necessary).

Still, we found careers cutting too much into family time. To prevent ourselves from becoming overly absorbed in our jobs, we decided, very formally, to set aside one evening a week for informal fun. Friday evening became "family night". From the time the kids were in first and second grade until they were 15 and 16 years of age (and didn't want us around anymore), we spent Friday evenings with them. We didn't restrict parent-child interaction to one night per week, but even in the midst of frenetic periods of on-the-job pressure the kids were guaranteed at least some special time with Mom and Dad. When there was "no time", we made some. If a "social" came up, we didn't go unless the kids could come along. Most often, however, they chose the activity (we had to see both *Care Bear* movies; we still bitterly resent that!).

Friday time together went a long way toward building and solidifying our family unit; it was good for the kids and good for us. Many years after we began our "family nights", we saw television spots (sponsored by a particular religious group), advocating essentially the same thing. In our view, that's the right idea. Many families "grab" time together, but it's rare to institutionalize it so firmly and regularly. Family nights are wonderful for all kids, but they're especially necessary for ADHDers who miss out on so much else. Quite simply, quality time is the most important commodity parents have to give.

Sharing

One would hope that a great deal of sharing, of one kind or another, takes place in "all of the above". However, we do see sharing as a somewhat distinct ingredient. Children need confidants with whom to share their disappointments, their dreams, and their aspirations. Parents, in part, can fill that role.

Amber gave off little fidgety hints when she needed someone to talk with. Some things were best discussed with Mom (how to hit Dad up for even more money); others with "wussy" Dad (how to make Mom relax the rules); others with both of us (how to deal with her obnoxious brother). At such times, Mom took her shopping, or Dad went out with her for a car ride—just so she had her sharing time with one of us.

During sharing time, we listened reflectively to the kids (yes, Chris got to vent about his obnoxious sister as well). We tried to focus on what they were saying, and mirror back their feelings by responding in an empathic, open-ended manner (cf. Dinkmeyer & McKay, 1976). With Amber's hyper discourse, you really have to listen hard to make head or tail of what's going on. But because we listened hard, she shared. And because she shared so openly, even as a young child, we knew what was going on inside her head (and could intervene to avert disaster). Eventually, Amber began to listen effectively herself. With all that speaking and listening experience, she has now become a very sensitive communicator in her own right.

Not-So-SMART Parenting

Without intending to sound alarmist, we suggest that when families do not provide the essential supports or elements for building relationships, young people often seek them elsewhere. If kids don't get variety and special moments, if they don't feel accepted, if there's no time for them, and if they have no one to talk to, they will likely look for substitutes. Some of our youth find what they're missing in gangs; others in drugs.

Take smoking marijuana as an example. Young people engaged in the activity may feel that it's a special occasion, where they are accepted in a spirit of camaraderie. It may give them a break or respite from pressure or boredom; after all, it's against the law and, therefore, exciting. And smoking dope certainly allows adolescents to spend time with "friends" in a caring or pseudo-caring environment. Sharing is there in abundance: witness how the smokers pass little butts from hand-to-hand in a ritualistic sharing ceremony. Smoking up has it all; all the ingredients to perpetuate the activity (and to lead to more serious ones). Although there are no surefire safeguards in today's world, the best way to prevent bad things from happening is by using SMARTS (or comparable approaches) to make good things happen.

PROGNOSIS

We're often asked about the outlook for hyper children. Despite pessimism in the literature, we remain guardedly optimistic. Basically, the answer to the question, "What is the prognosis for an ADHD child?" is "It depends."

The Downside

It is true that longitudinal data aren't always encouraging (Lambert, 1988; Weiss & Hechtman, 1993). Many ADHD children run into trouble in adolescence and adulthood. In Whalen and Henker's (1991) words, the prognosis in general is "far from benign". Because they're different (and have trouble fitting in and following the rules), ADHDers are often subjected to punishment. Gradually, the message may filter through that they are bad or worthless. Further, because of their impulsivity, questionable social skills, and tendency to lie, these youngsters often have trouble making and keeping friends. Isolation and loneliness result. To further exacerbate the situation, because of their attentional problems, overactive children usually don't do well at school. In a society where so much value is placed on academic success, they often see themselves as failures.

It's clear that one of the primary dangers for ADHD children is the almost constant assault on self-image. With Amber, one of our greatest challenges was to help her feel that, despite her problems, she was a worthwhile, valuable person. In schools, unfortunately, we have seen overactive children who were virtually beaten down by the time they reached junior high; many became frustrated, negative, and rebellious. Their self-concepts were shredded, to the point where it was nigh on impossible to pick up the pieces. Although we use humor and stress the positives in this book, much of the time it wasn't at all funny. Elsewhere, the second author has discussed the dark side of ADHD in more depth (McCluskey, McCluskey, McCluskey, & McCluskey, in press).

Amber, today, tells poignant stories about how devastated she was by various childhood incidents: being "uninvited" to birthday parties, never being allowed to go on field trips because of her disruptive in-class behavior, and receiving only two Valentine's Day cards in an elementary classroom made up of 21 students (McCluskey & McCluskey, 1999). The loss of school outings was particularly galling to us, for the field trip experience was one of the few things Amber might have handled well. She learned best by running, doing, and experimenting, yet the only field trips she went on were the ones we provided. It became a bit of a chore for us to keep replacing all the school outings that had been taken away, but we did so faithfully. Our reward was that Amber learned a great deal and behaved well, albeit exuberantly, during these make-up sojourns.

A Positive Spin

That being said, we deem it essential to put a positive spin on the situation (and believe us, with ADHDers, you do spin). Our inclination is, as much as possible, to look on the bright side. ADHD children can do very well, and become happy, productive adults—if the right things happen along the way. Consider this: some pundits have suggested that Albert Einstein, Mozart, Leonardo da Vinci, Cher, Henry Winkler, John Lennon, Winston Churchill, Jules Verne, Thomas Edison, George Patton, Whoopi Goldberg, Dustin Hoffman, Louis Pasteur, Tom Smothers, Beethoven, and Sylvester Stallone all suffered because of attention deficit or learning disorders. They did okay. Learning Disabilities Associations across the continent tell us that hyperactive individuals may possess acute powers of observation, a keen sense of humor, and the ability to view things from a unique perspective. Other positive traits associated with ADHD include sensitivity, empathy, originality, spontaneity, intensity, loyalty, and openness. It cannot be considered firmly established by any means, but—as stated in chapter 2—several researchers suggest that ADHD and creativity may, at times, go hand in hand (Cramond, 1994; Cramond, Gollmar, & Calic, 1994; Hartmann, 1997). Think of the possibilities for talented hyper people in the theatrical, artistic, althletic, and entrepreneurial domains.

Hartmann (1995) has presented several ADHD success stories. Nadeau (1996), highlighting the pluses of living life in an exhilarating "fast forward" mode, has also offered many hopeful accounts about how hyperactive individuals, from college students to senior citizens, have adapted and turned the condition to their advantage. While Nadeau stressed the need for counseling, medication, and other interventions to help the process along in some cases, large numbers of ADHDers learn to cope and live full, productive lives. Nadeau (1997) and Solden (1995) also emphasize the need to accept and enjoy ADHD, and put the positive side of it to good use in the home and in the workplace.

Back in the time of the hunters and gatherers (the good old days for hyperactive people), the ADHDers would have won! In today's structured world, though, they are at a disadvantage. Perhaps it is true that ADHD is seen as a "disorder" only because of our present social context. Clearly, school—a relatively recent development in the overall scheme of things—causes all kinds of problems for overactive, inattentive children, adolescents, and adults. But since these individuals have to live in the here and now, it may often be necessary to intervene and provide support.

Hartmann (1997), theorizing hyperactivity might simply be a normal, albeit extreme point on the continuum of human behavior, actually spoke of "hunters and farmers", and speculated that the high energy ADHD people are the descendants of hunters. Obviously, it wouldn't be easy being a hunter in the modern world. A highly speculative conceptualization, perhaps, but one that helps us take a different view and appreciate the strengths of sometimes marginalized members of our society.

A partial solution to the dilemma is for ADHDers to find things that suit them. With respect to education, they might consider selecting courses or programs to fit their style, be it in childcare, computer science, industrial arts, cosmetology, sales, photography, music, theater, or any other of the fine arts. In the workplace, Hartmann (1997) recommends ADHDers avoid 9:00-5:00 desk jobs. Might not some hyperactive individuals become sought-after cartoonists, writers, physiotherapists, park and recreation workers, or private detectives?

To revisit the heredity-environment issue briefly, we advocate taking a nurturing perspective, and doing our best to change situations to make them more accommodating for those with attentional problems. This is not to say we would allow ADHDers to do whatever they want; it's more to suggest that we should arrange things to give them a fighting chance.

We had an extraordinarily long-term plan for Amber, and we weren't all that disturbed by short-term failures. When she was retained in grade 6, we didn't panic. And since she had been part of the planning for years, she wasn't distraught either. It was just another step (albeit a step in place rather than forward) on the road. Some secondary teachers looked askance at us when we didn't worry about Amber's failures in their high school courses. Not knowing the big picture, they couldn't recognize that we were still celebrating the fact that she had arrived there at all. When you've been told your child is "schizophrenic", "severely learning disabled", "functionally illiterate", "psychopathically hyperactive", and "the worst child in the school", a failure or two in some senior high subjects doesn't seem all that devastating. We were, and still are, congratulating ourselves on the progress, not bemoaning tiny setbacks.

We're saddened by parents who see their children as representatives of the family and describe them as good or bad depending on the grades they receive. Amber can't get straight A's, but she can still be a good, worthwhile person. That she fails at something matters very little; we were concerned only if she stopped trying. Educators often forget there's more to life than academics. Schooling is very important to us, but family, friends, health, travel, and sports are relevant as well. We take pride in the academic, athletic, and work-related accomplishments of our two kids. We take more pride in the fact that they are positive, kind to others, and happy.

With Amber, we tried to instill the ancient Greek notion of the "golden mean", exposing her to a little bit of everything. We hope she will sample academics, languages, the arts, theater, sports, travel, and whatever else fancy dictates. When special talents and interests are identified, it's good to specialize, but it's also nice to complement specialization with a solid global perspective.

Popular wisdom used to suggest that hyperactivity would subside and disappear over time. While we're sure that this sort of thing may occur on occasion (biochemical changes in adolescence may alter and improve the condition for some), that hasn't precisely been the experience of most individuals we've observed, including Amber. Quite the opposite: the majority of active children we've followed longitudinally have turned into active adults. For most of them, ADHD has proven to be a long-haul disorder requiring long-term interventions. More and more literature is looking at hyperactivity from the womb to the tomb, rather than as a child-specific phenomenon (Fisher & Beckley, 1998; Goldstein, 1997; Hallowell & Ratey, 1994; Kelly & Ramundo, 1993; Nadeau, 1996, 1997; Wender, 1987).

To us, adolescence and young adulthood open up untold possibilities for ADHDers, if they can reach those stages emotionally intact. As a person grows from childhood to adolescence to adulthood, we feel it becomes easier to understand, control, and channel hyperactive tendencies or predispositions. Because what is negative in childhood may evolve into something highly positive later in life, it may at times be necessary to refocus, reframe, or recast reality. Think of it this way: is it not a small step from stubbornness in childhood to determination later in life, from inattentive daydreaming to creative invention, or from bullying to leadership? A difficult, overactive child can grow into an adult whose high energy level is universally admired. Some hyperactive individuals make excellent consultants, scurrying about the country with vigor and enthusiasm.

Recent Updates: Amber as a Young Adult

More than five years have come and gone since we last recounted our story (McCluskey & McCluskey, 1996); it's time for an update. In most ways, Amber has continued to improve and refine her coping strategies. Once allowed the occasional opportunity to take oral tests and recite to teachers while moving, she finally managed to pass dreaded biology and complete high school. You haven't seen anything until you've seen the "photosynthesis shuffle" and the "dance of the reproductive system".

Amber continues to arrange and rearrange furniture. When she lived with us, we dared not enter our home in the dark, for fear of hitting a chair, table, or sofa that wasn't where it had been mere hours before. Now, as a young wife and mother ensconced in her own place, Amber's repositioning of inanimate objects has actually increased. Her husband Corey, finally reacting to stubbed toes, has now asked that she rearrange the house no more than once a week! We, on the other hand, no longer have to worry about furniture: in a moment of impetuous generosity, Amber gave away our entire living room suite before moving out.

Together, Corey and Amber have channeled their energy into some positive directions. She worked rapidly with him, side by side, to fix up their little starter home. They sold at a profit and bought, and really spruced up, a pleasant, much larger house. And now that she is in demand as a speaker on the topic of ADHD, Amber has to wait her turn and sit through many long sessions. She has refined her doodling and counting of lights, chairs, and floor and ceiling tiles to the point where she can remain relatively settled for quite a spell. Other strengths have also emerged.

Problems, of course, still abound. Amber's math skills remain abysmal. She can't, for example, play a "quick" game of cribbage. Driving, a major issue for many ADHD adolescents and adults (Melmed, 2001), continues to be a real worry for us. Amber usually pays attention behind the wheel, but "little slips" occur every now and again. It's no wonder we're not entirely sanguine unless trustworthy friends or relatives accompany her.

There have been many amusing ADHD-related incidents of late. A year or so after her high school graduation, Amber—with our blessing—attempted to join the Royal Canadian Mounted Police. She came close, missing the cut-off grade on the entry examination by a mere couple of points (we expect due to her math). Slipping into our role of supportive parents, and consoling her as best we could after she had opened the Manila envelope containing the "devastating news", we were shocked to find Amber giggling hysterically at us. Her words, emitted between unrestrained chuckles, gave us pause: "You're both supposed to be intelligent people. What were you thinking? How could you have let me apply? Think about it. ADHD and a gun?" No second application was submitted. (We found out afterward that, in preparation for her training, Amber had accidentally shot Corey with a pellet gun during target practice! That's probably when she realized law enforcement wasn't the route for her—a young woman of intuition, we'd say.)

"IT WAS JUST A SERIES OF SIMPLE MISHAPS- THE LADY SNEEZED, THE BABY CRIED, THE DOG BARKED, MY GUN WENT OFF, THE HORSES STAMPEDED, AND THE PARADE ENDED IN RECORD TIME."

Every now and again, Amber still reacts without thinking. While eight-and-a-half-months pregnant with her daughter Hunter, she was in the midst of a relaxing bath in our comfortable tub. Abruptly, however, things became too quiet—our loud ceiling fan had been shut off. Since it turns on and off automatically with the single light switch, and since the light definitely remained on, we wondered what had transpired. "What are you doing?" we yelled. We were stunned by Amber's whispered reply: "Oops, I shouldn't have done that." Sure enough, naked, soaking wet, and almost ready to give birth, she had climbed out of the tub, up on top of the sink, and pulled the plug from the electrical outlet. Not good planning, to say the least.

We concur with those who say that ADHD is a lifelong condition. Its form may change and evolve, but with Amber it certainly has not disappeared. This was made even more obvious to us in May, 1997, when her daughter Hunter was born. Although we insisted that Amber go to prenatal classes prior to the "event", the information had limited impact. As usual, she didn't pay attention. Immediately after the birth, the doctor took the baby, and he and the nurses fussed over the tiny newcomer for a few minutes. Finding herself momentarily alone, Amber—thinking she was done—grabbed her I.V. pole, swiveled off the bed, and slipped away to get a sandwich. Her actions caused some consternation, especially since she had ignored some minor details (like delivering the placenta). We should have warned the medical staff, but who would have thought? Still, we can't say we were totally surprised when we heard a panic-stricken voice on the public address system: "Amber McCluskey, please report back to Birthing Room #2 immediately!" The second time around, in August of 2000 when Amber was having her son Easton, we noticed she was receiving very special care: there was a nurse with her every second. When we glanced at her chart, the reason became clear. The doctor had written in red, "Don't leave this patient. She may go!"

Even as she became a more confident, up-and-coming young lady, Amber's behaviors continued to be hard on her father. Although her motives were usually pure, she still managed to get poor old Dad into trouble on a regular basis. A case in point. Rather late in life for a major career change, Dad resigned from his administrative position in the school system to take up a professorship in the Education Program at the University of Winnipeg. The move was exciting, but not without its irritations. Due to communication and ordering mix-ups, there were major

delays in getting his computer shipped in and ready to go. After a couple of months without a desktop, an eternity in the publish-or-perish university environment, Dad's frustration was beginning to show. He was phoning questions down to "Tech Services" on almost a daily basis: "Has my Power Mac arrived yet?" "Can you call the supplier again?" "Once it gets here, how long will it take to set up?" The "techies", no doubt feeling somewhat harassed, assured him over and over again that they would get the machine delivered and online as quickly as possible.

At the time, Amber was starting to become quite a popular speaker on the ADHD scene. In an effort to make an Education Today group lecture come alive, her father invited the budding 23-year-old orator to address the entire array of first-year students. However, nothing is simple with Amber. Since other audiences had been paying for her time, she decided that a substantial honorarium should be forthcoming. With no budget for that sort of thing, Dad suggested that Amber show her gratitude for his years of suffering by offering a "freebie". Animated discussion followed. In the end, a compromise of sorts was reached, whereby Dad bought his ADHD daughter a spanking new university sweatsuit from the campus bookstore just prior to the presentation. Amber was delighted; so much so that in typically impulsive fashion, she accompanied the neophyte professor into his office, closed the door, and began to change with last-minute speed into the outfit that she now simply had to wear for the occasion.

Wouldn't you know it, a techie, wheeling the long-coveted computer, arrived and knocked loudly at the precise moment Amber started to disrobe! Amber opened the door just a crack, casually poked her head out, and announced: "Can you wait a minute until I'm finished getting dressed?" Her befuddled Dad, seated behind his desk, didn't immediately grasp the implications of what was taking place (though, as he walked arm in arm with his daughter to the lecture theater, he did notice the techie eyeing him with renewed respect). The next day, belatedly realizing Amber might well have ended his university career before it had begun, he made several important phone calls of clarification.

OH, HI! YOU CAN BRING THE EQUIPMENT IN AS SOON AS I GET DRESSED!

Spawn

You've heard the expression, "What goes around comes around!" It's true! Amber's little girl Hunter has just turned four, and, in many respects, she's the mirror image of her mother (though smarter!). Easton, Corey and Amber's baby son, is happy, calm, serene, and always laughing: he must have figured out who his parents are. Hunter, though, is Amber #2.

We savored a fairly recent occurrence involving Hunter that brought us back to when a very young Amber drove a psychiatrist to distraction by coloring the waiting room walls. Unlike her mother, Hunter has shown signs of precocity from an early age, reaching most developmental milestones extremely early, and speaking well by the time her first birthday rolled around. At only 18-months, this little one, who had learned to hit the redial button, put in an emergency telephone call to us. The conversation, chronicled in a previous publication (McCluskey, 2000c, p.9), went something like this:

> "Papa?" (that would be the first author).
> "Hi Hunter. How are you doing?"
> "Papa loves Hunter!"
> "Of course I do, but why are you phoning me?"
> "Daddy angry Hunter."
> "Why is Daddy mad at Hunter?"
> "Hunter color walls!"

Yes, like mother, like daughter; Hunter is definitely exhibiting many of Amber's behavior patterns. As a two-year old, she attempted to rid herself of an unwelcome guest who was competing for attention in her home. Hunter met the letter-carrier on the front porch and asked him if he'd mind taking her cousin Kailynd, an infant at the time, away in his bag. A climber as well, Hunter repeatedly attempted to elude us one day at our local zoo so that she might climb down and pet the alligator. Yup, she definitely needs watching. Fortunately, this girl has a mother who can keep up.

Just before Hunter turned three, she was the cause of an amusing incident at university. We had promised to take her to the movies, and in her unrestrained excitement, our "runner" broke away from Gramma in the hall and burst in upon Grampa's lecture to a third-year education class. She wanted to go "right now", but Grampa, standing her up on the desk at the front of the room, calmly explained that he had to finish with the students first. The following conversation ensued:

"Papa, what are you doing with these people?"

"Well, Hunter, I'm teaching them their ABCs."

At that point, the mischievous imp scanned the room deliberately, from left to right and then back again, before announcing: "Papa, it looks like a lot of them are going to have trouble!"

Yes, Hunter is an original. But it wouldn't do not to mention the other grandchildren. Easton's personality is beginning to emerge—he's a winning little guy. And Chris and Kari's daughters are truly special. Kristjana, the eldest at seven, is a remarkable reader who delights in her visits to university, her craft sessions with Gramma, and her "dates" with Grampa. Kailynd, a two-year-old, mischief-making, little devil in her own right, has latched on to Grampa (and, in precocious fashion as well, mastered the valuable arts of stone throwing and head butting). Kadynce, who at one year of age particularly loves being cuddled by Gramma, shows early signs of musical talent—her organ recitals and arias are vibrant (and loud). And all three of the girls, together with their cousin, have a great time riding in our car and singing along with Peter, Paul, and Mary. (Our predilection for '60s folk music notwithstanding, one can only listen to *Leaving on a Jet Plane, The Hammer Song,* and *Puff the Magic Dragon* so many times!) We must now restrain ourselves from writing further about Chris, Kari, and their brood—this really is not the place. However, in an earlier article about the importance of grandparent involvement (How does the title *Gray Matters* grab you?), and in other forthcoming pieces, we discuss their "very together" family in more detail (McCluskey & McCluskey, 2000; McCluskey & McCluskey, in press; McCluskey, McCluskey, McCluskey, & McCluskey, in press).

Getting back on track, parents often ask us what they can do to help hyperactive kids emerge from childhood unscathed and fulfill their potential later in life. We have two final suggestions:

Highlight the Positives

There is a need for more optimism in the world today. We ought to be searching for the best in all children and take the attitude that they all can learn. They may not learn the same things at the same rate, but they can all learn something. Why not look at life optimistically and view all kids in the best possible light? As parents and educators, it is obligatory to emphasize the positive.

Allow us some flashbacks. One incident in Amber's childhood caused us to look at her very differently, and much more optimistically. At the end of the school year when Amber was nine years of age, we were in bleak despair. We knew she was incredibly limited academically and had been told on numerous occasions that her behavior was past redemption. Discouraged, we decided to pack up, hop in our van, and drive for a family holiday way down south. (If you have an ADHDer and can manage it, buy a van. You can stick the child in the back and get some separation and breathing space for part of most journeys.) Mexico City was our destination of choice, largely because we have some extremely well-to-do, accommodating Mexican friends who are always willing to put us up for a couple of weeks. Much to our surprise, our hyperactive youngster—described by several educators as the worst of the worst—fit in without much trouble. Amber, clearly relishing the luxurious environment, took immediately to the upper-class style. She made friends for the first time in her life, and made them quickly. Our host summed it up wisely: "You Canadians and Americans. You're robots. This girl is alive! She's like us!"

The stay was enjoyable and invigorating. The Sunday prior to our return, all members of both families decided to head out to the market for a souvenir-hunting expedition. Amber, in an uncharacteristically subdued tone, surprised us by asking to stay back—a marked change in routine from someone who always wanted to be out and about. Because Sunday is, by tradition, the maids' day off, only one elderly cook, Dominga, was to remain behind. This compassionate soul graciously volunteered to babysit, and thinking that Amber might have a touch of Montezuma's revenge, we acquiesced to the scheme. Naturally, we should have known something devilish was afoot. Somehow, our nine-year-old had acquired enough Spanish during the brief visit to search through the Mexican telephone directory in our absence, identify a beauty salon, put in an "emergency" call, and make herself understood. Upon our return, we found that Amber had ordered a bevy of beauticians to the home. They were all busily engaged doing her hair, her nails, the works! The episode actually gave us a great deal of hope, for we marveled at the talent involved. We also appreciated the need to redirect it into more promising directions.

That's what we've continued to try with Amber. We don't sugarcoat the situation, but do endeavor to turn lemons into lemonade. Sometimes it's hard. Back in high school, Amber became friends with a young basketball player whose team had just returned from a trip to the States. As we were driving along together in our van, Amber asked him, "Where did you go?" He replied, "Pennsylvania." Amber responded, "Did you see any vampires?" Unable to make the connection, he could only look blankly back at her. We, on the other hand, knowing our daughter's geographical shortcomings, could watch his discomfiture and appreciate a moment of unholy ecstasy. She, in her off-base fashion, was thinking "Transylvania". Later, the young lad asked us, "Amber is very 'special', isn't she?" Taking it as a compliment, we agreed, but we don't really think that's what he had intended.

Although Amber has major flaws, the total package is still pretty neat. At home, we try to get her to acknowledge and work on the negatives, but also to appreciate her own strengths. Our hope is that she can learn to take the perspective articulated so well by Winston Churchill: "We are all worms, but I do believe I am a glow worm!"

Parents can do their overactive children a service by communicating some of their good traits to the school. Sadly, teachers often get bogged down in negatives when discussing ADHD students. And who can blame them? Parents, however, should help teachers refocus and consider the positives. Negative comments, made so often in staff rooms and elsewhere, should be discouraged. Positive ones should be highlighted. Also, rather than fight about every little thing, it is wise for parents and teachers to choose their encounters wisely. Before getting into a confrontation with Amber, the second author always asked herself, "Is this the hill I want to die on?" If it wasn't a crucial issue, she backed off a bit. Life, otherwise, would have become a constant battle.

From our admittedly biased perspective, we feel Amber has developed a number of the positive personality traits mentioned earlier. We've had enough of the bad over the years; our intent, henceforth, is to savor the good to the end of our days! We'll begin now by itemizing accomplishments and possibilities.

Amber is quick on the uptake. An example from her late teens: at a visit to our Red River Exhibition, she and Chris attended the Paul Bunyan Lumberjack Show (where competitive lumberjacks throw axes, saw, roll logs, and climb). During the climbing portion, the lumberjacks—with their legs protected by a type of brace or pad—scurry up 25-meter poles. After climbing one, they descend rapidly, and then rush, as quickly as possible, to start again on a second. As one poor fellow struggled awkwardly from pole to pole (the "braces" made it hard to navigate), Amber, forgetting herself, yelled out excitedly: "Run, Forrest, Run!" (If you missed the movie, you've missed the joke.) With this type of wit, might not Amber become a hit in certain social situations?

With her verbal skills and uninhibited nature, Amber does well in theater and drama. She is also adept at kinesthetic activities. Might we one day watch her perform with a community theater group? High-level basketball was once a possibility, but a knee injury has ended those prospects. However, Amber still plays for the sheer enjoyment of it, and she has dabbled as an assistant coach for a high school girls' team. Might she one day coach a team of her own?

Amber enjoys writing poems and singing. She has even written and performed a few songs in concerts with a local group. Might she end up a singer in a traveling band?

Amber, in certain situations, is very observant and attentive to fine detail. She likes filing and sorting, and she is beginning to develop her word processing and keyboarding skills on computer. Might we one day find her in an office setting? Meeting the public and handling reception duties would be no problem (believe us, she knows how to talk on the phone).

Amber has plenty of energy, vitality, and enthusiasm, which will stand her in good stead in interpersonal relationships and in the work force. We held on for years before we saw the energy channeled in productive directions, but that's beginning to happen more and more. If Amber can find the right setting, she has a contribution to make. And certainly, she'll brighten up almost any situation.

Amber has compassion. She'll stand up courageously for the underdog, and support her friends and family to the death. Might a career in the helping professions be a possibility? Amber's caring nature also shows through in the affection she lavishes on her pets. She truly has a way with animals. A career in veterinary medicine likely isn't realistic (she'd have trouble with biology and math), but her love of animals can still bring great joy into her life, and into theirs. Might she perhaps acquire a small hobby farm somewhere down the line?

Amber is especially good with children. With her high energy level, she gets right in there, designing and playing games with the little ones. And believe us, there's not a child born on the face of this earth who can wear her out! Might a career in childcare or education be in the offing?

Amber has gradually come to realize she possesses real talent in this area: more and more, it looks like education is the direction she will take. After some intensive preparation, Amber fared well on the entry tests, and has been accepted into the Education Access Program at the University of Winnipeg. Like so many other ADHD individuals, it took a long time—into her mid-twenties—before she felt confident enough to attempt such an undertaking. After so many aversive, scarring educational experiences as a child and adolescent, we're rather surprised our daughter has decided to take this path—for years following her grade 12 graduation, she swore she'd never go back to school of any kind. However, with maturity has come a new outlook. Remembering some of the mistakes that were made with her, Amber is now convinced she knows how to "treat kids right". While she is apprehensive, Amber is determined to follow in her brother's footsteps and become a teacher. We may finally have our revenge on the system!

Amber, despite her "faux pas propensity", has grown to be highly verbal, spontaneous, and articulate. Happily, her talent in this regard is being recognized and appreciated. Scorning preparation, she has "winged it" successfully as a keynote speaker at several major international events, including the Black Hills Seminars in Rapid City, the Ohio Prevention and Education Conference in Columbus, and the Council for Exceptional Children's Annual Convention in Kansas City. Amber has also received recent honors such as the *Aboriginal Youth Achievement Award* and the Learning Disabilities Association of Canada's *Beating The Odds Award*.

Even if she doesn't see her education through to completion, we're very proud our daughter has become a wonderful wife and mother. Corey has played a significant part in her growth. Several years older, and accustomed to providing support to a younger sister with special needs, he has been able to lend a patient, guiding hand. Amber's abundant energy and devotion to the children are touching. She does have to be restrained at times, however: she's the only mother we've ever seen who wakes the babies up to play!

To sum up, from a little girl who couldn't succeed at anything, Amber has grown into a young lady with a lot to offer. We're looking forward to seeing her gifts continue to evolve in the future.

Create a Vision

A body of literature stresses the importance of helping children and youth identify and develop their abilities and talents (Feldhusen, 1995; McCluskey, Baker, Bergsgaard, & McCluskey, 2001; McCluskey, Baker, O'Hagan, & Treffinger, 1995, 1998). When children are seen in a positive light, it helps them feel secure. When children learn to recognize their own talents, it builds confidence. And when children begin to develop their own talents, it helps them grow, persevere, and approach the future optimistically. Talent identification is dream-making; talent development reality-building. Together they help create a positive vision of the world.

For us, it is essential that adult caregivers begin to focus on "talent spotting" with all children, including those who are at risk (McCluskey & Treffinger, 1998). It can be hard. In the case of ADHDers, for example, behavior often masks ability: parents and teachers simply try to hang on, do damage control, and make it through to the end of the day. They don't always have time to seek out special abilities. Still, they must do their best to cast themselves in the role of "talent scouts" and look for the strengths.

Several made-in-Manitoba projects, put in place to serve at-risk populations, have made a pronounced difference to many young people (cf. McCluskey, Baker, Bergsgaard, & McCluskey, 2001; McCluskey, Baker, O'Hagan, & Treffinger, 1995, 1998). In these programs, Creative Problem Solving, mentoring, career awareness, and other interventions have been used successfully to reduce the recidivism rate of Native Canadian inmates, to reclaim talented but troubled high-school dropouts, and to support inner city children and youth at risk for alienation, school failure, and gang involvement. You can't really get populations much more at risk than these. Yet, in *Lost Prizes* and *Northern Lights*, two of the initiatives with school dropouts, the success rate is high—65% of these disenchanted, disenfranchised, disconnected students (who had been written off as delinquent ne'er-do-wells) returned to high school, entered post-secondary education programs, or obtained full-time employment. In a follow-up look at the data, it was found that more than half of the participants had, earlier in their lives, been referred by school personnel for a learning disability or ADHD. Such individuals were clearly capable of turning their lives around, but they needed a legitimate opportunity, plus concrete support for a considerable period of time.

We've always had a vision for Amber. However, had we told her teachers 15 years ago she would one day graduate from high school, be accepted into university, and become rather popular, they might have suggested the vision was a psychotic one. It wasn't: many positives have come to pass. And more are on their way!

We believe that, in large measure, life is what you make it. We've tried to plan for success for Amber. We were careful not to push too hard or have unrealistic expectations that would set her up for failure. Also, we never put all our eggs in one basket: if something didn't work out, there were always alternatives.

Even when the mere mention of school caused bleak despair, Chris and Amber believed they'd get into university sooner or later. While they were still very young, we bought into one of the university savings plans, complete with "scholarship" certificates for each of them. Those went on their bedroom walls. In junior high, when some of Chris's older acquaintances were dropping out of high school, he came to us puzzled. Thinking that higher education was mandatory, he asked: "Can they do that?"

No matter what others more grounded in reality might have thought, Amber always looked at university as a possibility. Since grade 9, she felt she might even play college basketball. Those dreams helped her through some difficult high school years. Imagine receiving a letter (from a coach at Mayville State in North Dakota) which began: "I want you to know that I have been following your athletic success over the past couple of years and am most impressed with your ability as a basketball player. Here at Mayville State University we have taken great pride in recruiting outstanding student-athletes like you." For a struggling student in distress, what a godsend! That letter kept Amber going for years. And even after her injury, Mayville personnel continued to call, encourage, and offer support. Their positive view fit well with our own. Amber will likely never spend any time at Mayville State. But even if she doesn't, we owe the institution a debt for enlarging her vision, keeping her spirits high, and giving her something to work toward.

We've never viewed university as the only route; merely one of many options to consider. We'd be equally pleased if Amber found her way into languages, music, the arts, or an office setting. We don't care so much what she does, as long as she does it conscientiously, productively, and with enjoyment.

In Conclusion

We believe the prognosis for ADHD children can be excellent, if they receive the appropriate help during the journey. Those who are left to make their own way in the world often struggle terribly. With tangible, long-term support from parents, teachers, and significant others, however, ADHDers often blossom. The negatives can turn into positives.

We hope others can learn from our mistakes and our successes. Our journey is not yet done, but we're proud of what we've wrought and of who Amber has become. We haven't precisely attained nirvana, but we're well-satisfied.

Chris is now established with his own family and career, and Amber is about to take on the onerous wife/mother/student role. Brief empty-nest syndrome hit us for a spell, but then the grandchildren (and babysitting) came to liven our days. That's good, for after working so hard for so long coping with our daughter's ADHD, we didn't know how to handle peace and quiet. We missed the constant aggravation.

When all is said and done, we like to think of our lives being measured by a memory box into which we try to cram all our recollections of joy, humor, treasured incidents, and family happiness. Thanks in large part to Amber's boundless energy and unique style, our memory box is pretty full!

The family then (1982), and now
(Amber's wedding, 1999).

REFERENCES

Abikoff, H. (1991). Cognitive training in ADHD children: Less to it than meets the eye. *Journal of Learning Disabilities, 24*(4), 205–209.

Alexander-Roberts, C. (1994). *The ADHD parenting handbook: Practical advice for parents from parents.* Dallas, TX: Taylor Publishing.

Alexander-Roberts, C. (1995). *ADHD and teens: A parent's guide to making it through the tough years.* Dallas, TX: Taylor Publishing.

Amen, D. G. (1996). *A child's guide to attention deficit disorder (for boys and girls 5 to 11).* Fairfield, CA: MindWorks Press.

American Psychiatric Association (1968). *Diagnostic and statistical manual of mental disorders* (2nd ed.). Washington, DC: Author.

American Psychiatric Association (1980). *Diagnostic and statistical manual of mental disorders* (3rd ed.). Washington, DC: Author.

American Psychiatric Association (1987). *Diagnostic and statistical manual of mental disorders* (3rd ed., rev.). Washington, DC: Author.

American Psychiatric Association (1994). *Diagnostic and statistical manual of mental disorders* (4th ed.). Washington, DC: Author.

Anastopoulos, A. D., DuPaul, G. J., & Barkley, R. A. (1991). Stimulant medication and parent training therapies for attention-deficit hyperactivity disorder. *Journal of Learning Disabilities, 24*(4), 210–218.

Armbruster, B. B., & Brown, A. L. (1984). Learning from reading: The role of metacognition. In R. C. Anderson, J. Osborn, & R. J. Tierney (Eds.), *Learning to read in American schools* (pp. 273–281), Hillsdale, NJ: Erlbaum.

Armstrong, T. (1996). ADD: Does it really exist? *Phi Delta Kappan, 77*(6), 424–428.

Arnold, L. E. (1999). Treatment alternatives for attention-deficit/hyperactivity disorder (ADHD). *Journal of Attention Disorders, 3*(1), 30–48.

Barbe, W. B., & Petreshene, S. S. (1981). *Teaching reading skills: Visual, auditory, and kinesthetic activities.* Columbus, OH: Zaner-Bloser.

Barkley, R. A. (1989). Attention deficit-hyperactivity disorder. In E. J. Mash & R. A. Barkley (Eds.), *Treatment of childhood disorders* (pp. 39–72). New York: Guilford Press.

Barkley, R. A. (1991). *Attention-deficit hyperactivity disorder: A clinical workbook.* New York: Guilford Press.

Barkley, R. A. (1998). *Attention-deficit hyperactivity disorder: A handbook for diagnosis and treatment* (2nd ed.). New York: Guilford Press.

Barkley, R. A. (2000). *Taking charge of ADHD: The complete, authoritative guide for parents* (2nd ed.). New York: Guilford Press.

Barrell, J. (1991). *Teaching for thoughtfulness.* New York: Longman.

Bastable, R. G., Laferriere, S., & Kolodie, I. (1995). Confronting and resolving conflict. In K. W. McCluskey, P. A. Baker, S. C. O'Hagan, & D. J. Treffinger (Eds.), *Lost prizes: Talent development and problem solving with at-risk students* (191–201). Sarasota, FL: Center for Creative Learning.

Bateson, G., Jackson, D. D., Haley, J., & Weakland, J. H. (1956). Toward a theory of schizophrenia. *Behavioral Science, 1*, 251–264.

Begun, R. W. (1995). *Social skills curriculum activities library.* Columbia, MO: Hawthorne.

Berry, C. A., Shaywitz, S. E., & Shaywitz, B. A. (1985). Girls with attention deficit disorder: A silent minority? A report on behavioral and cognitive characteristics. *Pediatrics, 76*, 801–809.

Block, M. A. (1996). *No more Ritalin: Treating ADHD without drugs.* New York: Kensington Books.

Breggin, P. (1998). *Talking back to Ritalin.* Monroe, ME: Common Courage Press.

Brendtro, L. K., Brokenleg, M., & Van Bockern, S. (1990). *Reclaiming youth at risk: Our hope for the future.* Bloomington, IN: National Educational Service.

Brophy, J. (1985). Teacher-student interaction. In J. B. Dusek (Ed.), *Teacher expectancies* (pp. 303–328). Hillsdale, NJ: Erlbaum.

Brophy, J., & Good, T. (1974). *Teacher-student relationships: Causes and consequences.* New York: Holt, Rinehart & Winston.

Cantwell, D. P., & Baker, L. (1991). Association between attention deficit-hyperactivity disorder and learning disorders. *Journal of Learning Disabilities, 24*(2), 88–95.

Carey, W. B. (1990). Should educators accept medical jargon? *Clinical Pediatrics, 29*(3), 193–194.

Carlson, G. A., & Rapport, M. D. (1989). Diagnostic classification issues in attention-deficit hyperactivity disorder. *Psychiatric Annals, 19*(11), 576–583.

Carroll, J. M. (1989). *The Copernican plan: Restructuring the American high school.* Andover, MA: The Regional Laboratory for Educational Improvement of the Northeast and the Islands.

Chilcoat, H. D., & Breslau, N. (1999). Pathways from ADHD to early drug use. *Journal of the American Academy of Child and Adolescent Psychiatry, 38*(11), 1347–1362.

Children and Adults with Attention Deficit Disorders (CH.A.D.D.). (Ed.). (1996). *ADD and adolescence: Strategies for success from CH.A.D.D.* Plantation, FL: Author.

Clark, L. (1989). *The time-out solution: A parent's guide for handling everyday behavior problems.* Chicago, IL: Contemporary Books.

Clements, S., & Peters, J. (1962). Minimal brain dysfunctions in the school-age child. *Archives of General Psychiatry, 6*, 185–197.

Conners, C. K. (1980). *Food additives and hyperactive children.* New York: Plenum.

Conners, C. K. (1997). *Conners rating scales - revised (CRS-R).* North Tonawanda, NY: Multi-Health Systems.

Conners, C. K. (1999a). *Conners adult ADHD rating scales (CAARS).* North Tonawanda, NY: Multi-Health Systems.

Conners, C. K. (1999b). *Conners continuous performance test.* North Tonawanda, NY: Multi-Health Systems.

Conners, C. K., & Wells, K. C. (1986). *Hyperkinetic children: A neuropsychosocial approach.* Newbury Park, CA: Sage.

Connolly, T., Dowd, T., Criste, A., Nelson, C., & Tobias, L. (1995). *The well-managed classroom: Promoting student success through social skill instruction.* Boys Town, NE: Boys Town Press.

Connor, J. P. (1974). *Classroom activities for helping hyperactive children.* New York: The Center for Applied Research in Education.

Consilia, M. (1978). *The non-coping child: A handbook for the teacher of the failing child.* Novato, CA: Academic Therapy Publications.

Corkum, P. V., & Siegel, L. S. (1993). Is the continuous performance task a valuable research tool for use with children with attention-deficit/hyperactivity disorder? *Journal of Child Psychology and Psychiatry, 34*, 1217–1239.

Council for Exceptional Children. (1992). *Children with ADD: A shared responsibility.* Reston, VA: Author.

Cramond, B. (1994). Attention-deficit hyperactivity disorder and creativity — What is the connection? *Journal of Creative Behavior, 28*(3), 193–210.

Cramond, B., Gollmar, S., & Calic, S. (1994). *The cross-identification of ADHD and creative children.* Paper presented at the National Association of Gifted Children Conference, Salt Lake City, UT.

Crenshaw, T. M., Kavale, K. A., Forness, S. R., & Reeve, R. E. (1999). Attention-deficit/hyperactivity disorder and the efficacy of stimulant medication: A meta-analysis. In T. Scruggs & M. Mastropieri (Eds.), *Advances in learning and behavioral disabilities* (Vol. 13). Greenwich, CT: JAI Press.

Crook, W. G. (1977). *Can your child ... read? Is he ... hyperactive? "Food" may be the villain.* Jackson, TN: Professional Books.

Curwin, R. L. (1999). *Building the spirit of hope.* Paper presented at the Black Hills Seminars, Spearfish, SD.

DeBruyn, R. L., & Larson, J. L. (1984). *You can handle them all: A discipline model for handling over one hundred different misbehaviors at school and at home.* Manhattan, KS: The Master Teacher.

DeGrandpre, R. (1999). *Ritalin nation: Rapid-fire culture and the transformation of human consciousness.* NY: W. W. Norton.

Diller, L. H. (1998). *Running on Ritalin: A physician reflects on children, society, and performance in a pill.* New York: Bantam Books.

Dinkmeyer, D., & McKay, G. D. (1976). *Systematic training for effective parenting: Parent's handbook.* Circle Pines, MN: American Guidance Service.

Dowd, T., & Tierney, J. (1992). *Teaching social skills to youth: A curriculum for child-care providers.* Boys Town, NE: Boys Town Press.

Dreikurs, R., & Grey, L. (1968). *A new approach to discipline: Logical consequences.* New York: Hawthorne.

Dunn, R., & Dunn, K. (1978). *Teaching students through their individual learning styles: A practical approach.* Englewood Cliffs, NJ: Prentice-Hall.

Dunn, R., Dunn, K., & Treffinger, D. J. (1992). *Bringing out the giftedness in your child.* New York: Wiley.

DuPaul, G. J., & Stoner, G. (1994). *ADHD in the schools: Assessment and intervention strategies.* New York: Guilford Press.

Dykman, K. D., & Dykman, R. A. (1998). Effect of nutritional supplements on attention-deficit/hyperactivity disorder. *Integrative Physiological and Behavioral Science, 33,* 49–60.

Dykman, R. A., & Ackerman, P. T. (1991). Attention deficit disorder and specific reading disability: Separate but often overlapping disorders. *Journal of Learning Disabilities, 24*(2), 96–103.

Eggen, P., & Kauchak, D. (1994). *Educational psychology: Classroom connections.* New York: Merrill.

Elliott, S. N., Kratochwill, T. R., Cook, J. L., & Travers, J. F. (2000). *Educational psychology: Effective teaching, effective learning* (3rd ed.). New York: McGraw-Hill.

Fachin, K. (1996). Teaching Tommy: A second-grader with attention deficit hyperactivity disorder. *Phi Delta Kappan, 77*(6), 437–441.

Fairchild, T. (1975). *Managing the hyperactive child in the classroom.* Austin, TX: Learning Concepts.

Feingold, B. (1975). *Why your child is hyperactive.* New York: Random House.

Feldhusen, J. F. (1995). *Talent identification and development in education: TIDE* (2nd ed.). Sarasota, FL: Center for Creative Learning.

Fischer, M., Barkley, R. A., Edelbrock, C. S., & Smallish, L. (1990). The adolescent outcome of hyperactive children diagnosed by research criteria: II. Academic, attentional and neuropsychological status. *Journal of Consulting and Clinical Psychology, 58*(5), 580–588.

Fisher, B. C., & Beckley, R. A. (1998). *Attention deficit disorder: Practical coping methods.* Boca Raton, FL: CRC Press.

Flavell, J. H. (1987). Speculations about the nature and development of metacognition. In F. E. Weinert & R. H. Klawe (Eds.), *Metacognition, motivation and understanding* (pp. 21–30). Hillsdale, NJ: Erlbaum.

Forman, S. G. (1993). *Coping skills interventions for children and adolescents.* San Francisco, CA: Jossey-Bass.

Forness, S. R., Kavale, K. A., & Crenshaw, T. M. (1999). Stimulant medication revisited: Effective treatment of children with ADHD. *Reclaiming Children and Youth, 7*(4), 230–233, 235.

Fowler, M. (1994). *Maybe you know my kid: A parents' guide to identifying, understanding and helping your child with attention-deficit hyperactivity disorder.* New York: Carol Publishing Group.

Frank, K., & Smith, S. J. (1994). *Getting a grip on ADD: A kid's guide to understanding and coping with attention disorders.* Minneapolis, MN: Educational Media Corporation.

Friedman, R. J., & Doyal, G. T. (1992). *Management of children and adolescents with attention deficit-hyperactivity disorder* (3rd ed.). Austin, TX: pro.ed.

Gadow, K. D. (1979). *Children on medication: A primer for school personnel.* Reston: VA: Council for Exceptional Children.

Gadow, K. D. (1988). Attention deficit disorder and hyperactivity: Pharmaco-therapies. In J. L. Matson (Ed.), *Handbook of treatment approaches in childhood psychopathology.* New York: Plenum Press.

Gadow, K. D., & Rapport, M. D. (1987). *Hyperactivity in school-aged children: Medical, psychological and educational management.* San Diego, CA: College-Hill.

Garber, S. W., Garber, M. D., & Spizman, R. F. (1995). *Is your child hyperactive? Impulsive? Distractible? Helping the ADD/hyperactive child.* New York: Villard Books.

Garber, S. W., Garber, M. D., & Spizman, R. F. (1996). *Beyond Ritalin: Facts about medication and other strategies for helping children, adolescents, and adults with attention deficit disorders.* New York: Villard Books.

Gardner, H. (1983). *Frames of mind: The theory of multiple intelligences.* New York: Basic Books.

Garshowitz, E. A., Hui, F., Levinson, H. N., Lyon, M., & Marshall, D. (2001). *The all-in-one guide to ADD and hyperactivity.* Niagara Falls, NY: AGES Publications.

Gaynor, J. (1990). Attention deficit disorder may be etched in sand. *Beyond Behavior, 2*(1), 17–18.

Gehret, J. (1991). *Eagle eyes: A child's guide to paying attention.* Fairport, NY: Verbal Images Press.

Gibbs, J. C., Potter, G. B., & Goldstein, A. P. (1995). *The EQUIP program: Teaching youth to think and act responsibly through a peer-helping approach.* Champaign, IL: Research Press.

Ginott, H. G. (1969). *Between parent and child: New solutions to old problems.* New York: Avon Books.

Glasser, W. (1978). *Ten steps to discipline.* Hollywood, CA: Media Five.

Goldenberg, C. (1992). The limits of expectations: A case for case knowledge about teacher expectancy effects. *American Educational Research Journal, 29,* 517–544.

Goldstein, S. (1997). *Managing attention and learning disorders in late adolescence and adulthood: A guide for practitioners.* New York: John Wiley & Sons.

Goldstein, S., & Goldstein, M. (1986). *A parent's guide: Attention deficit disorders in children.* Salt Lake City, UT: Neurology, Learning and Behavior Center.

Goldstein, S., & Goldstein, M. (1987). *A teacher's guide: Attention deficit disorders in children.* Salt Lake City, UT: Neurology, Learning and Behavior Center.

Goldstein, S., & Goldstein, M. (1992). *Hyperactivity: Why won't my child pay attention?* New York: John Wiley & Sons.

Goldstein, S., & Goldstein, M. (1998). *Managing attention-deficit/ hyperactivity disorder in children: A guide for practitioners* (2nd ed.). New York: John Wiley & Sons.

Gordon, M. (1988). *The Gordon diagnostic system.* Dewitt, NY: Gordon Systems.

Gordon, M. (1991). *ADHD/hyperactivity: A consumer's guide for parents and teachers.* DeWitt, NY: GSI Publications.

Greenberg, G. S., & Horn, W. F. (1991). *Attention deficit hyperactivity disorder: Questions and answers for parents.* Champaign, IL: Research Press.

Greenberg, L. M. (1990). *Test of variables of attention (TOVA).* Los Alamitos, CA: Universal Attention Disorders.

Greenhill, L. L., & Osman, B. B. (1999). *Ritalin: Theory and practice* (2nd ed.). New York: Mary Liebert.

Gross, M. D., & Wilson, W. C. (1974). *Minimal brain dysfunction.* New York: Bruner/Mazel.

Hallowell, E. M., & Ratey, J. J. (1994). *Driven to distraction: Recognizing and coping with attention deficit disorder from childhood through adulthood.* New York: Touchstone.

Hancock, L. (1996, March 18). Mother's little helper. *Newsweek,* p. 51–56.

Hartmann, T. (1995). *ADD success stories: A guide to fulfillment for families with attention deficit disorder.* Grass Valley, CA: Underwood Books.

Hartmann, T. (1997). *Attention deficit disorder: A different perception* (2nd ed.). Grass Valley, CA: Underwood Books.

Hemphill, R. (1996). Secondary school transition: Planning for success. In Children and Adults with Attention Deficit Disorders (CH.A.D.D.). (Ed.). *ADD and adolescence: Strategies for success from CH.A.D.D.* (pp. 45–48). Plantation, FL: Author.

Hollands, E. (1983). *How a mother copes with hyperactivity.* Altona, MB: Anny Book.

Ingersoll, B. D. (1988). *Your hyperactive child: A parent's guide to coping with attention deficit disorder.* New York: Doubleday.

Ingersoll, B. D., & Goldstein, S. (1993). *Attention deficit disorder and learning disabilities: Realities, myths and controversial treatments.* New York: Doubleday.

Isaksen, S. G., Dorval, K. B., & Treffinger, D. J. (2000). *Creative approaches to problem solving: A framework for change* (2nd ed.) Dubuque, IA: Kendall/Hunt.

Jacobs, E. H. (1998). *Fathering the ADHD child: A book for fathers, mothers, and professionals.* Northvale, NJ: Jason Aronson.

Jacobvitz, D., Sroufe, L. A., Stewart, M., & Leffert, N. (1990). Treatment of attentional and hyperactivity problems in children with sympatho-mimetic drugs: A comprehensive review. *Journal of the American Academy of Child and Adolescent Psychiatry, 29,* 677–688.

Johnson, D. D. (1992). *I can't sit still: Educating and affirming inattentive and hyperactive children.* Santa Cruz, CA: ETR Associates.

Johnson, H. C. (1988). Drugs, dialogue, or diet: Diagnosing and treating the hyperactive child. *Social Work, 33*(4), 349–355.

Johnson, H. C. (1989). The disruptive child: Problems of definition. *Social Casework, 70*(8), 469–478.

Kavale, K. (1982). The efficacy of stimulant drug treatment for hyperactivity: A meta-analysis. *Journal of Learning Disabilities, 15,* 280–289.

Kelly, K., & Ramundo, P. (1993). *You mean I'm not lazy, stupid or crazy?! A self-help book for adults with attention deficit disorder.* New York: Scribner.

Kendall, P. C., & Braswell, L. (1985). *Cognitive-behavioral therapy for impulsive children.* New York: Guilford Press.

Kennedy, P., Terdal, L., & Fusetti, L. (1993). *The hyperactive child book.* New York: St. Martin's Press.

Kinsbourne, M., & Caplan, P. J. (1979). *Children's learning and attention problems.* Boston, MA: Little, Brown & Company.

Kinsbourne, M., & Swanson, J. M. (1978). *Hyperactivity. Learning disabilities: Information please.* Montreal, PQ: Quebec Association for Children with Learning Disabilities.

Knights, R. M., & Bakker, D. J. (Eds.). (1980). *Treatment of hyperactive and learning disordered children: Current research.* Baltimore, MD: University Park Press.

Laferriere, S., Bastable, R. G., McCluskey, K. W., Anderson, D., & Torske, L. (1995). Risky business at the Regional Support Centre: A modified approach for at-risk students. In K. W. McCluskey, P. A. Baker, S. C. O'Hagan, & D. J. Treffinger (Eds.), *Lost prizes: Talent development and problem solving with at-risk students* (pp. 77–92). Sarasota, FL: Center for Creative Learning.

Lambert, N. M. (1988). Adolescent outcomes for hyperactive children: Perspectives on general and specific patterns of childhood risk for adolescent educational, social, and mental health problems. *American Psychologist, 43,* 786–799.

Lantieri, L., & Patti, J. (1996). *Waging peace in our schools.* Boston, MA: Beacon Press.

Lapouse, R., & Monk, M. (1958). An epidemiological study of behavior characteristics in children. *American Journal of Public Health, 48,* 1134–1144.

Learning Disabilities Association of Manitoba. (1999). *Working together: Home and school. Helping children with learning disabilities and attention deficit disorders ... succeed* (3rd ed.). Winnipeg, MB: Author.

Leavy, J. (1996, March 18). With Ritalin, the son also rises. *Newsweek,* p. 59.

Levine, M. D. (1987). *Explaining attention deficits to children. The concentration cockpit: Guidelines for its utilization.* Cambridge, MA: Educators Publishing Service.

Long, N. J. (1997). The therapeutic power of kindness. *Reclaiming Children and Youth, 5*(4), 242–246.

Long, N. J., Wood, M. M., & Fecser, F. A. (2001). *Life space crisis intervention* (2nd ed.). Austin, TX: pro.ed.

Lubar, J. F. (1991). Discourse on the development of EEG diagnostics and biofeedback for attention-deficit/hyperactivity disorders. *Biofeedback and Self-Regulation, 16,* 201–225.

Manos, M. J., Short, E. J., & Findling, R. L. (1999). Differential effectiveness of methylphenidate and adderall in school-age youths with attention-deficit/hyperactivity disorder. *Journal of the American Academy of Child and Adolescent Psychiatry, 38*(7), 813–819.

Marks, D. J., Himelstein, J., Newcorn, J. H., & Halperin, J. M. (1999). Identification of AD/HD subtypes using laboratory-based measures: A cluster analysis. *Journal of Abnormal Child Psychology, 2*(2), 167–175.

Martin, C. A., Welsh, R. J., McKay, S. E., & Bareuther, C. M. (1984). Hyperactivity (attention-deficit disorder). *The Journal of Family Practice, 19*(3), 367–380.

Martin, G., & Pear, J. (1998). *Behavior modification: What it is and how to do it* (6th ed.). Upper Saddle River, NJ: Prentice-Hall.

Maslow, A. H. (1970). *Motivation and personality* (2nd ed.). New York: Harper and Row.

Maté, G. (1999). *Scattered minds: A new look at the origins and healing of attention deficit disorder.* Toronto, ON: Alfred A. Knopf Canada.

McCluskey, K. W. (1986, September). Optimism, personality, and education. *Canadian Education Association Newsletter,* 1 & 6.

McCluskey, K. W. (2000a). Lines in the sand: Are students with difficulties being forced from our schools? *Reaching Today's Youth, 4*(4), 28–33.

McCluskey, K. W. (2000b). Setting the stage for productive problem solving. In S. G. Isaksen (Ed.), *Facilitative leadership: Making a difference with creative problem solving* (pp. 77–101). Dubuque, IA: Kendall/Hunt.

McCluskey, K. W. (2000c, March). The importance of being early: A case for preschool enrichment. *Parenting for High Potential,* 8–13.

McCluskey, K. W., & Albas, D. C. (1981). Perception of contradictory speech by normal and disturbed children at various age levels. *Journal of Abnormal Psychology, 90*(5), 490–493.

McCluskey, K. W., Baker, P. A., Bergsgaard, M., & McCluskey, A. L. A. (2001). *Creative problem solving in the trenches: Interventions with at-risk populations.* The Monograph Series. Buffalo, NY: Creative Problem Solving Group—Buffalo.

McCluskey, K. W., Baker, P. A., O'Hagan, S. C., & Treffinger, D. J. (Eds.). (1995). *Lost prizes: Talent development and problem solving with at-risk students.* Saras FL: Center for Creative Learning.

McCluskey, K. W., Baker, P. A., O'Hagan, S. C., & Treffinger, D. J. (1998). Recapturing at-risk, talented high-school dropouts: A summary of the three-year lost prizes project. *Gifted and Talented International, 13*(2), 73–78.

McCluskey, K. W., & McCluskey, A. L. A. (1996). *Butterfly kisses: Amber's journey through hyperactivity.* Queenston, ON: Marvin Melnyk Associates.

McCluskey, K. W., & McCluskey, A. L. A. (1999). The agony and the empathy: A hyperactive child's journey from despair to achievement. *Reclaiming Children and Youth, 7*(4), 205–211.

McCluskey, K. W., & McCluskey, A. L. A. (2000). Gray matters: The power of grandparent involvement. *Reclaiming Children and Youth, 9*(2), 111–115.

McCluskey, K. W., & McCluskey, A. L. A. (in press). From at-risk to enriched in the inner city: The role of parents and grandparents. In D. Sutherland, S. Hart, and L. Sokal (Eds.), *Resilience and capacity building in inner city learning communities.* Winnipeg, MB: Portage & Main Press.

McCluskey, A. L. A., McCluskey, K. W., McCluskey, C. I., & McCluskey, A. A. (in press). *ADHD: A family affair.* Winnipeg, MB: Portage & Main Press.

McCluskey, K. W., & Treffinger, D. J. (1998). Nurturing talented but troubled children and youth. *Reclaiming Children and Youth, 6*(4), 215–219, 226.

McCluskey, K. W., & Walker, K. D. (1986). *The doubtful gift: Strategies for educating gifted children in the regular classroom.* Kingston, ON: Ronald P. Frye.

McCormick, C. B., & Pressley, M. (1997). *Educational psychology: Learning, instruction, assessment.* New York: Longman.

Melmed, R. (2001). *Recent advances in attention deficit hyperactivity disorder (ADHD).* Paper presented at the Annual Conference of the Council for Exceptional Children, Kansas City, MO.

Minde, K. K. (1988). *A guide for parents on hyperactivity in children.* Ottawa, ON: Learning Disabilities Association of Canada.

Moghadam, H. (1988). *Attention deficit disorder: Hyperactivity revisited.* Calgary, AB: Detselig Enterprises.

Moghadam, H., & Fagan, J. (1994). *Attention deficit disorder: A concise source of information for parents and teachers* (2nd ed.). Calgary, AB: Detselig Enterprises.

Moragne, W. (1996). *Attention deficit disorder.* Brookfield, CT: The Millbrook Press.

Moss, R. A. (1990). *Why Johnny can't concentrate: Coping with attention deficit problems.* New York: Bantam Books.

Murphy, V., & Hicks-Stewart, K. (1991). Learning disabilities and attention deficit-hyperactivity disorder: An international perspective. *Journal of Learning Disabilities, 24*(7), 386–388.

Nadeau, K. G. (1994). *Survival guide for college students with ADD or LD.* New York: Magination Press.

Nadeau, K. G. (1996). *Adventures in fast forward: Life, love, and work for the ADD adult.* New York: Bruner/Mazel.

Nadeau, K. G. (1997). *ADD in the workplace: Choices, changes, and challenges.* Bristol, PA: Bruner/Mazel.

Naglieri, J. A., & Das, J. P. (1997). *Das-Naglieri cognitive assessment system (CAS).* Itasca, IL: Riverside.

Nash, D., & Treffinger, D. J. (1993). *The mentor.* Waco, TX: Prufrock Press.

Noller, R. B. (1982). *Mentoring: A voiced scarf.* Buffalo: NY: Bearly Limited.

Noller, R. B., & Frey, B. R. (1994). *Mentoring: An annotated bibliography (1982–1992).* Sarasota, FL: Center for Creative Learning.

Noller, R. B., & Frey, B. R. (1995). Mentoring for the continued development of lost prizes. In K. W. McCluskey, P. A. Baker, S. C. O'Hagan, & D. J. Treffinger (Eds.), *Lost prizes: Talent development and problem solving with at-risk students* (pp. 203–221). Sarasota, FL: Center for Creative Learning.

Nylund, D. (2000). *Treating Huckleberry Finn: A new narrative approach to working with kids diagnosed ADD/ADHD.* San Francisco, CA: Jossey-Bass.

O'Brien, M., & Obrzut, J. (1986). Attention deficit disorder with hyperactivity: A review and implications for the classroom. *Journal of Special Education, 20,* 281–297.

Osborne, S. S., Kosiewicz, M. M., Crumley, E. B., & Lee, C. (1987). Distractible students use self-monitoring. *Teaching Exceptional Children, 19*(2), 66–69.

Oud, M . C. (1988). *You can manage any schoolchild! The complete guidebook for coping with hyperactive and problem children in the classroom.* Vancouver, BC: EduServ.

Paolitto, A. W. (1999). Clinical evaluation of the cognitive assessment system with children with ADHD. *The ADHD Report, 7*(4), 1–5.

Parker, H. C. (1988). *The ADD hyperactivity workbook for parents, teachers, and kids.* Plantation, FL: Impact Publications.

Parker, H. C. (1992). *The ADD hyperactivity handbook for schools: Effective strategies for identifying and teaching ADD students in elementary and secondary schools.* Plantation, FL: Impact Publications.

Phelan, T. W. (1991). *1-2-3 magic: Training your preschoolers and preteens to do what you want.* Glen Ellyn, IL: Child Management.

Phelan, T. W. (1993). *All about attention deficit disorder. Symptoms, diagnosis and treatment: Children and adults.* Glen Ellyn, IL: Child Management.

Pliszka, S. R., Browne, R. G., Olvera, R. L., & Wynne, S. K. (2000). A double-blind, placebo-controlled study of adderall and methylphenidate in the treatment of attention-deficit/hyperactivity disorder. *Journal of the American Academy of Child and Adolescent Psychiatry, 39,* 619–626.

Potashkin, B. D., & Beckles, N. (1990). Relative efficacy of Ritalin and biofeedback treatments in the management of hyperactivity. *Biofeedback and Self-Regulation, 15,* 305–315.

Quinn, P. O. (1995). *Adolescents and ADD: Gaining the advantage.* New York: Magination Press, 1995.

Quinn, P. O., & Stern, J. M. (1991). *Putting on the brakes: Young people's guide to understanding attention deficit hyperactivity disorder (ADHD).* New York: Magination Press.

Rapport, M. D., Tucker, S. B., DuPaul, G. J., Merlo, M., & Stoner, G. (1986). Hyperactivity and frustration: The influence of size and control over rewards in delaying gratification. *Journal of Abnormal Psychology, 14,* 192–204.

Renzulli, J. S. (1994). *Schools for talent development: A practical plan for total school improvement.* Mansfield Center, CT: Creative Learning Press.

Rief, S. F. (1993). *How to reach and teach ADD/ADHD children: Practical techniques, strategies, and interventions for helping children with attention problems and hyperactivity.* West Nyack, NY: The Center for Applied Research in Education.

Roberts, J. A. F. (1967). *An introduction to medical genetics.* London: Oxford University Press.

Robin, A. L. (1998). *ADHD in adolescents: Diagnosis and treatment.* New York: Guilford Press.

Robinson, F. (1972). *Effective study.* New York: Macmillan.

Rogers, C. R. (1951). *Client-centered therapy.* Boston, MA: Houghton Mifflin.

Rosenthal, R., & Jacobson, L. (1968). *Pygmalion in the classroom*. New York: Holt, Rinehart & Winston.

Safer, D. J., & Allen, R. P. (1976). *Hyperactive children: Diagnosis and management*. Baltimore, MD: University Park Press.

Safer, D. J., & Krager, J. M. (1994). The increased rate of stimulant treatment for hyperactive/inattentive students in secondary schools. *Pediatrics, 94,* 462–464.

Schmidt, M. H., Mocks, P., Lay, B., Eisert, H. G., Fojkar, R., Fritz-Sigmund, D., Marcus, A., & Musaeus, B. (1997). Does oligoantigenic diet influence hyperactive/conduct-disordered children?—A controlled trial. *European Child and Adolescent Psychiatry, 6,* 88–95.

Schwartz, S., & Johnson, J. H. (1987). *Psychopathology of childhood: A clinical-experimental approach* (2nd ed.). New York: Pergamon.

Schwarzbeck, C. (1994, September 18). Hyperactivity haunts father. *Winnipeg Free Press*, p. C2.

Seidel, W. T., & Joschko, M. (1990). Evidence of difficulties in sustained attention in children with ADHD. *Journal of Abnormal Child Psychology, 18*(2), 217–229.

Sheppard, R. (1998, September). Growing Up Hyperactive, *Maclean's*, p. 45–46.

Silver, L. B. (1990). Attention-deficit hyperactivity disorder: Is it a learning disability or a related disorder? *Journal of Learning Disabilities, 23,* 394–397.

Silver, L. B. (1992). *The misunderstood child: A guide for parents of children with learning disabilities* (2nd. ed). New York: TAB Books.

Smelter, R. W., Rasch, B. W., Fleming, J., Nazos, P., & Baranowski, S. (1996). Is attention deficit disorder becoming a desired diagnosis? *Phi Delta Kappon, 77*(6), 429–432.

Solden, S. (1995). *Women with attention deficit disorder: Embracing disorganization at home and in the workplace*. Grass Valley, CA: Underwood Books.

Stein, D. B. (1999). *Ritalin is not the answer: A drug-free, practical program for children diagnosed with ADD or ADHD*. San Francisco, CA: Jossey-Bass.

Stephens, T. M. (1992). *Social skills in the classroom* (2nd ed.). Odessa, FL: Psychological Assessment Resources.

Stevens, W. H, & McCluskey, K. W. (1998). *Strategies for desperate parents: Managing the challenges of attention deficit and misbehavior* (2nd ed.). Queenston, ON: Marvin Melnyk Associates.

Strauss, A. A., & Lehtinen, L. E. (1947). *Psychopathology and education for the brain-injured child.* New York: Grune and Stratton.

Swanson, J. M., Cantwell, D. P., Lerner, M., McBurnett, K., & Hanna, G. (1991). Effects of stimulant medication on learning in children with ADHD. *Journal of Learning Disabilities, 24*(4), 219–230, 255.

Szatmari, P., Offord, D. R., & Boyle, M. H. (1989). Ontario child health study: Prevalence of attention deficit disorder with hyperactivity. *Journal of Child Psychology and Psychiatry, 30,* 219–230.

Taylor, E. A. (1986). Childhood hyperactivity. *British Journal of Psychiatry, 149,* 562–573.

Taylor, J. F. (1980). *The hyperactive child and the family.* New York: Dodd, Mead.

Taylor, J. F. (1990). *Helping your hyperactive child.* Rocklin, CA: Prima Publishing & Communications.

Taylor, J. F. (1996). Building conscience and self-control skills in children and adolescents with ADHD. In Children and Adults with Attention Deficit Disorders (CH.A.D.D.). (Ed.). *ADD and adolescence: Strategies for success from CH.A.D.D.* (pp. 65–66). Plantation, FL: Author.

Thompson, A. M. (1996). Attention deficit hyperactivity disorder: A parent's perspective. *Phi Delta Kappan, 77*(6), 433–436.

Train, A. (1996). *ADHD: How to deal with very difficult children.* London, England: Souvenir Press.

Treffinger, D. J. (1998). From gifted education to programming for talent development. *Phi Delta Kappan, 79*(10), 752–755.

Treffinger, D. J., Isaksen, S. G., & Dorval, K. B. (1994). *Creative problem solving: An introduction* (2nd ed.). Sarasota, FL: Center for Creative Learning.

Treffinger, D.J., Isaksen, S.G., & Dorval, K.B. (2000). *Creative problem solving: An introduction* (3rd ed.). Waco, TX: Prufrock Press.

Trites, R. L., Dugas, F., Lynch, G., & Ferguson, B. (1979). Incidence of hyperactivity. *Journal of Pediatric Psychology, 4,* 179–188.

Umansky, W., & Smalley, B. S. (1994). *ADD. Helping your child: Untying the knot of attention deficit disorder.* New York: Warner Books.

Valett, R. E. (1974). *The psychoeducational treatment of hyperactive children.* Belmont, CA: Fearon.

Vorrath, H. H., & Brendtro, L. K. (1985). *Positive peer culture.* Hawthorne, NY: Aldine de Gruyter.

Walker III, S. (1998). *The hyperactivity hoax: How to stop drugging your child and find real medical help.* New York: St. Martin's Press.

Weaver, C. (1994, May/June). Eight tips for teachers with ADHD students. *Instructor*, p. 43.

Weiner, I. B. (1982). *Child and adolescent psychopathology.* New York: John Wiley & Sons.

Weiss, G., & Hechtman, L. T. (1993). *Hyperactive children grown up* (2nd ed.). New York: Guilford Press.

Weiss, G., Hechtman, L., Milroy, T., & Perlman, T. (1985). Psychiatric status of hyperactives as adults: A controlled prospective 15-year follow-up of 63 hyperactive children. *Journal of the American Academy of Child and Adolescent Psychiatry, 24,* 211–220.

Wender, P. H. (1987). *The hyperactive child, adolescent, and adult. Attention deficit disorder through the lifespan.* New York: Oxford University Press.

Wender, P. H. (1995). *Attention-deficit hyperactivity disorder in adults.* New York: Oxford University Press.

Weyandt, L. L. (2001). *An ADHD primer.* Boston, MA: Allyn and Bacon.

Whalen, C. K., & Henker, B. (1991). Social impact of stimulant treatment for hyperactive children. *Journal of Learning Disabilities, 24*(4), 231–241.

Wodrich, D. L. (1994). *Attention deficit hyperactivity disorder: What every parent wants to know.* Baltimore, MD: Paul H. Brookes.

Zentall, S. S., & Meyer, M. J. (1987). Self-regulation of stimulation for ADD-H children during reading and vigilance task performance. *Journal of Abnormal Child Psychology, 15,* 519–536.

AUTHOR INDEX

SUBJECT INDEX